Excursions In Philosophical Logic

Excursions In Philosophical Logic

Peter K. Schotch

ISBN 978-0-9780552-2-6

Library and Archives Canada Cataloguing in Publication

Schotch Peter K
   Excursions In Philosophical Logic
   Peter K. Schotch

   Includes bibliographical references and index.
   ISBN 978-0-9780552-2-6

   1. Philosophical Logic 2. Formal Logic II. Schotch, Peter
K.

   BC71.S42 2006   160   C2006-901677-1

Contents

Acknowledgements

This work took many years to produce, not because I work slowly (although I often do) but because it represents some of the projects and problems upon which I have worked over the course of my career (so far). It is common in the acknowledgements section to say something about the people who helped along the way and I will not break with the tradition. There is however a problem—the list of those who have helped would take up the largest portion of the book! So I must needs pick and choose. If I leave out your name please don't feel slighted, you have my gratitude even so.

I first became interested in philosophical logic at the University of Waterloo, where J. Sayer Minas was my mentor and also my thesis advisor. My great debt to him remains even though my views on the nature of logic have changed in the years since, almost beyond recognition, from the ones he taught. *His* mentor, though not his thesis advisor (it's a long story) was C. West Churchman, a pioneer in modal logic who eventually left logic for a career in management science—a field of which he was one of the inventors. Churchman in his turn was a student of H.B. Smith at the University of Pennsylvania. Smith's accomplishments in logic, modal logic in particular remain almost unknown to this very day although a knowledgeable and unbiased historian might well count his contribution as comparable to that of his contemporary C.I. Lewis.

Many of my students have participated in the writing of this work, only some of them directly. In the latter group I would mention in particular Gillman Payette, Blaine d'Entremont, Judy Pelham, and Mary MacLeod. There were many and many of my students who simply asked for clarification when I failed to see that such was needed. Others pointed out typographical as well as intellectual mistakes.

In the latter class, two standouts were Julia Watt and Maia Jaakson. But every time I stepped into the lecture room, I stepped out having learned something about my subject. I can only hope that my students ended up learning more than I did.

But all that to the side, in order to write a book, even a relatively small one like this, one needs the desire to do such writing, and the space in which to do it. By the term "space" here, I mean not only a physical place to work and sufficient blocks of time to get the work done, but also a kind of acceptance. Many authors salute their families for 'putting up with them' while they wrote, and that is well and good; who among us is without the need to be put up with, now and then? But I mean more than that. My wife Cara has gone well beyond the stage of putting up with the writing me, and actively encourages and sustains it. Without her this book would not have been written; indeed it would not even have been possible to write it. In order to emphasize this, I dedicate the book to her.

Preface

This book is a monograph in the strict sense; but it is not really an introduction, nor is it a survey. It is intended to be a collection of resources, at least some of which would be useful in a course on philosophical logic. I have used the book in this fashion myself several times as have some of my friends and students. In some cases, the chapters are built upon a previously published article or articles—though I hasten to assure my prospective readers that the building in question required more than staples. In some cases the bones of the original work are hardly visible at all, while in every case the flesh has been extensively re-worked.

I have not attempted in this volume to collect all the different topics that have attracted my attention over the years. Instead I have tried to choose subjects which fit together well in order to represent my own view on how philosophical logic ought to be done. In some cases my way of doing things is relatively close to the mainstream, but in other cases the divergence is notable. It has long seemed to me that philosophical logic which emphasizes the logic at the expense of the philosophy, is an approach which is doomed to fail. To say such a thing seems un-called for—the sort of thing which "goes without saying." Alas it doesn't seem to go very far, at least in the standard literature.

One

Introduction

1.1 What is Philosophical Logic? Some Schools of Thought

The subject of this book is philosophical logic. This term has covered a multitude of sins, and covers at least a bunch, to this very day. At one time the adjective "philosophical" was taken to be a synonym for "informal" (or perhaps "not very formal"). For example, P.F. Strawson's *Introduction to Logic* was once taken to be the epitome of philosophical logic. The contrast used to be with "mathematical" which meant both formal and pertaining to metamathematics. This usage has declined (but not entirely vanished) and nowadays one is more liable to mean 'the sort of thing which is published in the *Journal of Philosophical Logic*.' While there is no doubt that one will typically find a lot more prose per cc in the JPL than in the *Journal of Symbolic Logic*, much of the work is as formal as anyone could wish. So what makes logic philosophical is its subject matter (at least in most cases).

And the subject matter in question is supposed to have something or other to do with philosophy. It often seems that this requirement is more honored in the breach. Em-

1

barrassingly often, the philosophy with which it is mainly concerned is philosophical logic. It works like this: Somebody launches a logical study of an existing branch of philosophy (which we might as well take to have nothing to do with logic directly). In this study certain tools are proposed to aid in the analysis—a certain type of already existing system of logic for instance. What happens next is that the tools become the main focus of further studies in this area, while the original application of the tools comes to occupy a smaller and smaller portion of the literature.

On the issue of what logic itself is supposed to be, however, we have an unparalleled unanimity. Logic is the science of reasoning. In this science, everyone recognizes a division between deductive logic and the rest (non-deductive, let's call it), which parallels a similar division in our informal notion of reasoning. This informal division can be characterized as follows: A piece of reasoning is deductive provided that if somebody were to accept the premises, that person would be bound, on grounds of rationality, to accept the conclusion. The science of logic has made great strides in formalizing deduction but has no similar success to report in the non-deductive arena (no strides at all, some would say). Certainly we shall confine ourselves, by and large, to deduction.

Having such a consensus on the foundations does not imply, unfortunately, that logicians everywhere are united on the means whereby to prosecute their science. In fact there are two great 'logical cultures' which we would do well to canvass before we embark upon our own studies. In the first culture, a piece of deductive reasoning (*a deduction*, as we shall say) is correct if and only if the steps by which we progress from the premises to the conclusion are, one and all, in accord with a (properly specified) set of *rules of inference* (or rules of *proof*). Those who recognize this as the central paradigm are said to be in the *proof-theoretic* or *syntactical* camp. In this paradigm, any sequence of steps which is rule-compliant is called a proof, and when the inference from a batch of premises to a conclusion is correct in this sense, the premises are said to prove the conclusion. Using Γ to represent the premise set and α to represent the conclusion, the notation $\Gamma \vdash \alpha$ represents that *gamma proves alpha*.

In the other culture, a deduction is correct if and only if it is *truth-preserving*, which is to say that one could never infer a false conclusion from true premises. This assumes that we have on hand some gloss on 'a sentence is true.' The provision of such can be problematic, but, in simple cases, these problems can be overcome (for the most part). Anyone who thinks that truth has a central role to play in defining correct (deductive) inference is said to be a *model-theorist* or to be influenced mainly by the *semantic* paradigm. When the inference from gamma to alpha is truth preserving, we say that *gamma entails alpha* and write: $\Gamma \vDash \alpha$.

Within both great traditions, there are many subdivisions which stem from disagreements and heresies regarding just what are and will be the correct rules of proof, the number and character of the truth-values, and many other occasions for contention and name-calling. At least one of these divisions is of interest because it cuts across the proof-theory/model-theory divide. The distinction in question is between the followers of Boole who believe that the central items of logical enquiry are sentences, and the followers of the angels (or of Aristotle anyway) who believe to the contrary that inferences (or arguments as some insist on calling the things, in spite of the unfortunate agonistic overtones of that term) are the heart and soul of logic. These divisions have no agreed-upon name, so we are free to baptize as we will, and we call the Boolean version the *laws of thought* tradition, and the Aristotelian one the *in-*

ferential tradition.

This division comes down to a difference over what are the "good-guys." In the laws of thought stream, the job of logic is to winnow the theorems (proof-theorists), or the logical-truths (model-theorists), from the chaff of the great mass of other formulas. On the inferential view, we try to demarcate the class of derivations or proofs if we are proof-theorists, and the class of valid inferences if not. A word of warning is in order here: logic is not chemistry. The terminology just introduced conforms, by and large, to current usage, but there are significant variations. Many logicians have a foot, or at least a toe, in both the proof-theory and model-theory camps, and these non-aligned folk often want some top-level notion to capture these ideas. So one sometimes sees the term 'logical-truth' used to denote a law of thought, in either semantic or syntactic guise. Similarly, one finds the term 'valid,' applied in this ambidextrous fashion to inferences. In these cases, since the model theoretic terms have been co-opted, new terminology must be fabricated. The term tautology can be dredged up to serve as the model-theoretic way of referring to a law of thought (for all that it has connotations of triviality), with entailment (or sometimes semantic entailment) doing duty on the inferential side.

1.2 Notation

In the object language we use $\supset$, $\equiv$, $\wedge$, $\vee$, $\neg$, and $\perp$ for the conditional, biconditional, conjunction, disjunction, negation, and falsum (or 'the false') respectively. Although we have a separate piece of notation for the biconditional, we don't normally regard it as 'primitive'; i.e. we usually regard it as an abbreviation for the conjunction of two conditionals. These "logical words" are often referred to as *connectives*, or nearly as often as *logical operators*. The latter term is usually shortened to *operators.*

In the metalanguage we use $\Rightarrow$, $\Leftrightarrow$, and & , for the conditional, biconditional, and conjunction, and various sorts of 'strikethrough' for negation, along with the word 'not.' For the syntactical consequence relation we normally use $\vdash$ (usually read 'proves'). When it becomes necessary to indicate different notions, we often use the 'turnstile' notation with superscripts or subscripts. For the semantic consequence relation we use the 'double-bar turnstile' $\vDash$ (usually read 'entails') with subscripts and superscripts again providing the means to distinguish different flavors of these, one from the other. It is often convenient to have some notation to represent the case in which every member of a set of sentences, e.g. Γ is proved by a certain set, e.g. Δ and we shall use $\Delta \vdash \Gamma$ to this effect. The knowledgeable reader should resist the inclination to take this expression as an assertion of some Gentzen-like formal system (of so-called *sequent logic* for instance.)

The familiar $\forall$ and $\exists$ do duty as the universal and existential quantifiers in both object and metalanguage (but in the latter, English words and phrases are also pressed into service). More exotic operators are introduced *in situ.* We assume the usual definition of well-formed expression and a member of that class will often be referred to as a *formula* but, for reasons of style, we sometimes call these objects *sentences* as well.[1]

When a formula contains no formula as a proper part or, alternatively, contains no operators, we say that it is an *atomic* formula. The set of such formulas will be referred to by means of **At**. In the usual application we shall be concerned with a subset of **At**, which subset will typically be referred to by I. Each such subset of **At** is called an *index*.

---

[1]A formula is, after all, merely a sentence of a formal language.

Lower case Greek letters are used for sentence variables, and capital Greek letters for sets of them, although other bits of notation are sometimes also used for sets in order to comply with the dictates of style or of mnemonicity. We use the standard 'set brace' notation, with $\{\alpha, \beta, \gamma\}$ representing the set containing as members just the sentences α, β and γ, while $\{\alpha\}$ is the unit-set of α, and $\{x|F(x)\}$ is an *abstract*, in this case the set of all items x, which have the property indicated by 'F.'

$\varnothing$ is the empty set, $\in$ is 'member of' and the operators $\cup$, and $\cap$ stand for set union and intersection respectively. While $\subseteq$ indicates the set relation of inclusion, $\subset$ represents proper inclusion. For relative complement, the \ notation is used, e.g. $\Gamma \backslash \Delta$ is the relative complement of delta in gamma (i.e. those members of gamma which are not members of delta).

Let Γ be a set of formulas, and ♥ a unary sentence operator, then:

$$♥[\Gamma] = \{♥\alpha | \alpha \in \Gamma\}, \text{ while}$$

$$♥(\Gamma) = \{\beta | ♥\beta \in \Gamma\}.$$

It is important to notice that these set operations of putting on heart operators, and stripping off heart operators are not inverses of each other. For while

$$♥(♥[\Gamma]) = \Gamma$$

it is not in general true that

$$♥[♥(\Gamma)] = \Gamma$$

In fact, the best we can do here is

$$♥[♥(\Gamma)] \subseteq \Gamma$$

since the result of ♥(Γ) is the set of formulas α, which in Γ, were of the form ♥α, but any formula in Γ which doesn't appear prefixed by ♥, does not appear in ♥(Γ).

Two

Classical Logic

Classical logic serves as a point of departure for most of philosophical logic, but that should not be taken as a sign that everybody has a perfectly definite idea of what classical logic is. Rather 'classical' is a vague predicate subject to degrees, and it often makes sense to speak of one logic being more classical than another. We shall take the position that there are certain hallmarks, and that if a logic accumulates enough of these then it is classical. We shall also talk about something called 'the classical perspective' which is equally vague but no less influential. In the following we give a brief account of the classical logic of sentences which we generally call *CSL*.

Proof-theory

It is one of the hallmarks of classical logic that proofs (or derivations) are finite sequences of steps. From this it follows that:

$$[C]\ \Gamma \vdash \alpha \implies (\exists \Delta)(\Delta \subseteq \Gamma\ \&\ \text{FINITE}(\Delta)\ \&\ \Delta \vdash \alpha)$$

which property of $\vdash$ is called *compactness*.

Our presentation of classical proof-theory will follow a notionally *natural deduction* line, since we expect many to have been exposed to such in previous logic courses, but we are not true-blue in this (as in so many other things). For one thing, we lay more emphasis on what are called *structural rules* than is thought healthy by the usual practitioners of natural deduction. An inference rule is called structural when it isn't an introduction or elimination rule, i.e. when it doesn't mention any operators. It is normal in natural deduction settings (especially for those in the so-called Fitch-style) to limp along with what purports to be a single such rule, often referred to as the *rule of reiteration*. We appeal to this rule whenever we 'bring down' some formula within the scope of which we are currently working, into the present subderivation. This, as it turns out, is actually a conflation of the following two rules:

$$[R] \; \alpha \in \Gamma \;\Rightarrow\; \Gamma \vdash \alpha$$
$$[M] \; \Gamma \vdash \alpha \;\Rightarrow\; \Gamma \cup \Delta \vdash \alpha$$

where the letters naming these are intended to suggest 'reflexivity' and 'monotonicity' respectively. When we bring down a formula inside the same subderivation we are using [R] and when we bring it down from 'above and to the left' we are actually using [M]. It is important not to confuse these since they are independent, and one's classical perspective might one day become so occluded, as to require that one of these rules hold without also the other (at least in unrestricted form).

The names we announce for these rules are different from their historical names. In the more general setting of Gentzen's sequent logic, [R] is usually stated as $\alpha \vdash \alpha$ and is referred to as *axiom*. What we call monotonicity, is usually called *dilution*.[1]

---

[1]Many people prefer to render the German word as 'thinning,' but I have been convinced that dilution is a better translation.

Both of the above form central parts of the classical suite (they are what we earlier called hallmarks, of classical logic), along with:

$$[T] \ (\Gamma, \alpha \vdash \beta \ \& \ \Gamma \vdash \alpha) \ \Rightarrow \ \Gamma \vdash \beta$$

where the expression 'Γ, α' abbreviates: $\Gamma \cup \{\alpha\}$.

This rule is named to suggest 'transitivity' though for historical reasons, it would have been better to refer to it as *cut*. A transitivity rule which looks more like an exemplar of that property is:

$$[T^*] \ ((\forall \beta)(\beta \in \Delta \ \Rightarrow \ \Gamma \vdash \beta) \ \& \ \Delta \vdash \alpha) \ \Rightarrow \ \Gamma \vdash \alpha$$

The latter rule may be derived from [T] with the aid of [M], which gives us at least some warrant to call [T] 'transitivity.' Finally we have a rather peculiar rule, which must be classified as structural because though it mentions operators, it neither introduces nor eliminates any. It should doubtless be regarded as a limiting case of a structural rule. We first require a piece of terminology.

We define the notion of an atomic formula being distinct from a formula, in the way one would expect

Definition 2.0.1. We say that an atomic formula α is *distinct from* a formula β if and only if α does not occur as a part of β.

[W] If $\alpha_1, \ldots, \alpha_m$ are all atomic, and distinct from $\beta_1, \ldots, \beta_n$, then:

$$(\{\alpha_1, \ldots, \alpha_m\} \vdash \beta_1 \vee \ldots \vee \beta_n) \ \Rightarrow \ (\beta_1 \notin \textbf{At} \ or \ \ldots \ or \ \beta_n \notin \textbf{At})$$

We refer to [W] as Wittgenstein's Law, for it says in effect that there are no inferential relations between distinct atomic sentences.

Where ♥ is some connective, we shall refer to its introduction rule by means of [♥I] and to ♥'s elimination rule with [♥E]. The following are the connective rules of classical logic:

First the introduction rules:

$$[\wedge I] \quad \Gamma \vdash \alpha \,\&\, \Gamma \vdash \beta \;\Rightarrow\; \Gamma \vdash \alpha \wedge \beta$$
$$[\vee I] \quad \Gamma \vdash \alpha \text{ or } \Gamma \vdash \beta \;\Rightarrow\; \Gamma \vdash \alpha \vee \beta$$
$$[\supset I] \quad \Gamma, \alpha \vdash \beta \;\Rightarrow\; \Gamma \vdash \alpha \supset \beta$$
$$[\bot I] \quad \Gamma \vdash \alpha \,\&\, \Gamma \vdash \neg\alpha \;\Rightarrow\; \Gamma \vdash \bot$$
$$[\neg I] \quad \Gamma, \alpha \vdash \bot \;\Rightarrow\; \Gamma \vdash \neg\alpha$$

The elimination rules:

$$[\wedge E] \qquad\qquad \Gamma \vdash \alpha \wedge \beta \;\Rightarrow\; \Gamma \vdash \alpha \,\&\, \Gamma \vdash \beta$$
$$[\vee E] \quad (\Gamma \vdash \alpha \vee \beta \,\&\, \Gamma, \alpha \vdash \gamma \,\&\, \Gamma, \beta \vdash \gamma) \;\Rightarrow\; \Gamma \vdash \gamma$$
$$[\supset E] \qquad\qquad \Gamma \vdash \alpha \supset \beta \,\&\, \Gamma \vdash \alpha \;\Rightarrow\; \Gamma \vdash \beta$$
$$[\bot E] \qquad\qquad\qquad \Gamma \vdash \bot \;\Rightarrow\; \Gamma \vdash \alpha$$
$$[\neg E] \qquad\qquad\qquad \Gamma, \neg\alpha \vdash \bot \;\Rightarrow\; \Gamma \vdash \alpha$$

For conjunction (invariably the 'nicest' operator) we can combine the elimination and introduction rules into the single rule:

$$[\wedge]\ \Gamma \vdash \alpha \wedge \beta \;\Longleftrightarrow\; \Gamma \vdash \alpha \,\&\, \Gamma \vdash \beta$$

Each of the operator rules is one of our hallmarks. If a logic has all of these rules, then it has the classical perspective on the operators. Does this mean that it is classical logic? Not necessarily, for the logic in question may fail to have all of the classical structural rules. But what if a logic has all the classical rules of both flavors—wouldn't it then be classical? Many would say yes. We certainly would say yes. But not everybody would. There is a version of the classical perspective, the *narrow* version we call it, according to which a logic is classical if it has all and only the classical rules, and the classical operator set. We shall encounter this species of tunnel-vision elsewhere in the text where it will receive a more extended treatment.

Model Theory

The model theory of classical logic is based on the notion of an *truth-value assignment*, which is a function v, mapping the set of atomic formulas **At**, into the set of truth values $\{0, 1\}$.

In most actual deployments of the theory we restrict our attention to some subset I of **At** which we refer to as an *index*. To say this is to say that we mostly consider languages built up out of the atoms belonging to I. Such languages will be indicated by subscripting with the index in question, after the manner of SL_I. When no confusion will result, we often omit the subscript. Given this restriction we may define truth-value assignments along the lines of

For each index I and $i \subseteq I$

Definition 2.0.2. $v_i(\alpha) = 1$ for every $\alpha \in i$, and
$v_i(\beta) = 0$ for every $\beta \in I \setminus i$.

The class of all assignments relative to an index I (or *spanning I*) is indicated by $\mathbb{V}_I$.

This definition ensures that a truth-value assignment is a *function*. This is to say first, that every member of I is assigned a value because every member of I is either a member of i or not (this is called the totality condition) and second, that no member of I receives more than one value since I and $I \setminus i$ are disjoint (this is called the single-valuedness condition).

That assignments are functions is another of the hallmarks of classicality. The totality condition means that, from the classical perspective, there are no truth-value gaps

for atomic sentences; sentences that is, which fail, for whatever reason, to be evaluated. The single-valuedness condition means, given that we have two truth-values interpreted as falsehood (0) and truth (1), that no atomic sentence can be both true and false. It is important to notice
here what the functionality of assignments does *not* imply
that sentences are two-valued.

One finds many authors suggesting that the number of
truth-values is an important part of the classical perspective, but this is false. It is easy to find a logic which obeys
all (and only) the classical structural and operator rules,
but has more than two values (in fact it follows from the
tradition begun by Boole, that such a logic could have 4, 8,
16,..., 2^n,... values, or even infinitely many).

It certainly *is* part of the classical perspective however,
that the evaluation of compound formulas inherits the totality and single-valuedness conferred upon their atomic
brethren by assignments. This is guaranteed in the definition of the truth-predicate: *true with respect to the assignment* v_i, written: '$v_i \vDash$'. This predicate is defined recursively as follows:

(Basis)

$$v_i \vDash \alpha \iff v(\alpha) = 1 \text{ for all } \alpha \in i \subseteq I$$

(Recursion clauses)

$$[T\wedge]\ v_i \vDash \alpha \wedge \beta \iff v_i \vDash \alpha \,\&\, v_i \vDash \beta$$
$$[T\vee]\ v_i \vDash \alpha \vee \beta \iff v_i \vDash \alpha \text{ or } v_i \vDash \beta$$
$$[T\supset]\ v_i \vDash \alpha \supset \beta \iff (v_i \vDash \alpha \implies v_i \vDash \beta)$$
$$[T\bot]\ \forall i \subseteq I : v_i \nvDash \bot$$
$$[T\neg]\ v_i \vDash \neg\alpha \iff v_i \nvDash \alpha$$

In the recursive part of this definition, the clauses labeled [$T\wedge$] etc. are often known as *truth-conditions*. Given

that every assignment v_i is required to be a function, and that the recursion clauses cover all possible compounds, this recursively defines a total predicate, i.e. one that is defined for every formula. In like manner, given that the definition is recursive, a compound formula can receive more than a single value only if one of its component atomic formulas does—which is to say that it cannot, so long as assignments are functional.

We call any scheme for extending a predicate from the atoms of some index I to all formulas built up out of those atoms *truth-functional* provided it satisfies the above truth conditions. It is relatively easy to show that truth-functional extensions are unique.

Theorem 2.0.3. *Let X and Y be two truth-functional extensions of $i \subseteq I$, in other words: for every $\alpha \in I$: $X(\alpha) \iff Y(\alpha) \iff \alpha \in i$. It follows that for every formula β (in the language built up from the index I), $X(\beta) \iff Y(\beta)$.*

Proof. This result follows at once from the fact that for any formula α, if two predicates like X and Y disagree on α, they must disagree on at least one subformula of α. □

Now for the important definition, *semantic entailment*:

Definition 2.0.4.
$$\Gamma \vDash \alpha \iff (\forall v \in \mathbb{V})(v \vDash \Gamma \implies v \vDash \alpha)$$

Here we are treating '$v \vDash \Gamma$' as an abbreviation for '$(\forall \beta \in \Gamma)(v \vDash \beta)$,' which is to adopt the classical gloss on 'the premises are true'— namely that 'each individual premise is true.' This is another hallmark of classical logic.

We mustn't forget to define logical truth as well (for all those supporters of the laws of thought). It is a special case of the definition just given:

Definition 2.0.5. $\vDash \alpha \iff (\forall v \in \mathbb{V})(v \vDash \alpha)$

It is easy to see that this amounts to $\varnothing \vDash \alpha$.

Theories

A theory is a set of sentences which is deductively closed—i.e. it contains everything that it proves. To put this formally:

Definition 2.0.6.
THEORY$(\Delta) \iff (\forall \alpha)(\Delta \vdash \alpha \implies \alpha \in \Delta)$

This turns out to be reasonably close to our informal account of a theory as an organized body of knowledge, which is an important idea. The formal counterpart is at least as important. It is certainly important enough for us to introduce an operator (sometimes called a deductive closure operator) that makes theories out of sets:

Definition 2.0.7. $\mathbb{C}_\vdash(\Gamma) = \{\alpha | \Gamma \vdash \alpha\}$

Having this operator allows us to give an alternative definition of a theory for classical theories at least, viz. as *fixed-points* under the $\mathbb{C}_\vdash$ operator:

Definition 2.0.8. THEORY$(\Delta) \iff \mathbb{C}_\vdash(\Delta) = \Delta$

It is not a trivial observation that the alternative is equivalent to the original definition, and in fact some recourse to the classical structural rules is required to demonstrate this.

The best way to think of theories (given rule [R]) is as sets for which provability is the same thing as membership, for not only do they contain all they prove, but they also prove all that they contain. That is a nice property. We now make a list of properties that seem to us also to be nice. They are, in fact the properties that a theory would enjoy if it were also a truth-functional extension of some $i \subseteq I$, where I is an index.

Definition 2.0.9. CON(Δ) $\iff$ $\Delta \nvdash \bot$

Definition 2.0.10.
CONJ(Δ) $\iff$ $(\Delta \vdash \alpha \land \beta \iff \Delta \vdash \alpha \,\&\, \Delta \vdash \beta)$

Definition 2.0.11.
PRIME(Δ) $\iff$ $(\Delta \vdash \alpha \lor \beta \iff \Delta \vdash \alpha \text{ or } \Delta \vdash \beta)$

Definition 2.0.12.
IMPLIC(Δ) $\iff$ $((\Delta \vdash \alpha \supset \beta) \iff (\Delta \vdash \alpha \implies \Delta \vdash \beta)$

Definition 2.0.13. COMP(Δ) $\iff$ $(\forall \alpha)(\Delta \vdash \alpha \text{ or } \Delta \vdash \neg \alpha)$

All these properties at least *look* reasonable. If you take a poll in an introductory logic class, almost everybody will vote for the complete slate—in fact, a very high percentage of these same folk assume that theories already have these properties, since they assume that arbitrary sets (let alone

theories) have them. Unfortunately, these untutored intuitions turn out to be wrong. Classical theories have only the
conjunctive property (which is possessed also by arbitrary
sets).

Informally, if a theory, Δ, were inconsistent in the sense
that CON(Δ) fails (i.e. if it proved 'the false'), then we would
discard it; it wouldn't be a proper theory at all. But we
have to allow the existence of improper theories or suffer
a mangling of our account. There is this to make up for
inconsistency: since inconsistent theories prove everything
(given the negation rules), they at least enjoy all the other
properties on the list.

But how can we construct these theories which are also
truth-functional extensions? This turns out to be straightforward.

$\mathbb{D}_i$, the *diagram of $i \subseteq I$* is defined:

Definition 2.0.14. $\mathbb{D}_i = \{\alpha \in i\} \cup \{\neg\beta \mid \beta \in I \,\&\, \beta \notin i\}$

In other words the diagram of some $i \subseteq I$ is the set
of all atomic sentences in i (the ones that i 'claims to be
true') together with the set of the negations of the atomic
sentences which belong to the index I but not to i (the ones
that i 'claims to be false').

Informally, the diagram of a set $i \subseteq I$ is a set which
'says' that all of the atomic formulas in i are provable (by
virtue of rule [R]) and that for every other atomic formula
in the index I, that negation of that formula is provable.
One sometimes says that a set like $\mathbb{D}_i$ *decides $i \subseteq I$*. We
shall refer to the class of all diagrams spanning the index
I by means of $\mathbb{D}_I$. We shall refer to $i \subseteq I$ as the *positive
component* of the diagram $\mathbb{D}_i$. The set of negated atomic
formulas which ensures that the diagram spans all of I will
be referred to as the *negative component* of $\mathbb{D}_i$.

We shall refer to the deductive closure $\mathbb{C}_\vdash(\mathbb{D}_i)$ by T_i. It is also known as the *theory of i*.

$\mathbb{T}_I$, the *indexed class of theories spanning SL_I*, is defined:

Definition 2.0.15. $\mathbb{T}_I = \{T_i | i \subseteq I\}$

The first thing to notice is that we can assure ourselves that for every index I and $i \subseteq I$, $\mathbb{D}_i$ is consistent. This is assured by our principle [W]. If the diagram were not consistent then:

$$\{\alpha | \alpha \in i\} \cup \{\neg\beta | \beta \notin i \,\&\, \beta \in I\} \vdash \perp$$

Since derivations are of finite length there must be some finite number of the β formulas which suffice to prove $\perp$. Say there are n of them,

$$\{\alpha | \alpha \in i\} \cup \{\neg\beta_1, \ldots, \neg\beta_n\} \vdash \perp$$

by classical reasoning then

$$\{\alpha | \alpha \in i\} \vdash (\neg\beta_1 \wedge \ldots \wedge \neg\beta_n) \supset \perp \text{ and so}$$

$$\{\alpha | \alpha \in i\} \vdash \neg(\neg\beta_1 \wedge \ldots \wedge \neg\beta_n) \text{ which is to say that}$$

$$\{\alpha | \alpha \in i\} \vdash (\beta_1 \vee \ldots \vee \beta_n)$$

But in this case since the α's are distinct from the β's (no atomic formula can both belong and not belong to i) [W] assures us that some of the β formulas must be non-atomic, which is impossible.

Given the consistency of $\mathbb{D}_i$, the consistency of T_i follows right away. If $\perp$ can be deduced from the consequences of some underlying set (in this case the diagram of i) the structural rule [T] assures us that $\perp$ can be deduced from that same set.

It will turn out that T_i has the properties after which we hankered above, namely primeness, completeness, and implicativity. Let's start with completeness. We wish to show that, for every index I and $i \subseteq I$:

$$[\text{COMP}] \ T_i \vdash \neg\alpha \iff T_i \nvdash \alpha$$

The $\implies$ direction of this we have at once from the propriety (consistency) of T_i, so we need only provide a proof of the right-to-left ($\impliedby$) direction.

Lemma 2.0.16. *For every index I and $i \subseteq I$: $T_i \nvdash \alpha \implies$ $T_i \vdash \neg\alpha$*

Proof. We see at once[2] that the completeness property must hold for the atomic formulas of I on the definition of $\mathbb{D}_i$. Suppose now for reductio that there is a formula α, of SL_I such that $T_i \nvdash \alpha$ and $T_i \nvdash \neg\alpha$. We shall say in this case that T_i *fails to decide* α. We now proceed by cases.

> $[\alpha = \beta \wedge \gamma]$ If $T_i \nvdash \beta \wedge \gamma$ then it must be the case that either $T_i \nvdash \beta$ or $T_i \nvdash \gamma$ (otherwise T_i would prove the conjunction after all). On the other hand, since $T_i \nvdash \neg(\alpha \wedge \gamma)$ it must be the case that $T_i \nvdash \neg\beta \vee \neg\gamma$ but that can only happen in case $T_i \nvdash \neg\beta$ and $T_i \nvdash \neg\gamma$. From all of this it follows that if T_i fails to decide a conjunction then it must fail to decide a conjunct. the remaining cases,
>
> $[\alpha = \beta \vee \gamma]$
>
> $[\alpha = \beta \supset \gamma]$
>
> $[\alpha = \neg\beta]$

are left as an exercise.

In each case then, the failure of T_i to decide a formula α results in a similar failure for a (proper) subformula of α. Since all formulas are of finite length, it follows that

---

[2]This argument was pointed out to me by Gillman Payette.

if there were any formula which is not decided by T_i, there would be an atomic formula which is not decided by T_i. But since T_i is defined to be the closure of a diagram, it must decide every atomic formula in I. □

Corollary 2.0.17. [T_i is complete] *For every index I and $i \subseteq I$*

$$T_i \vdash \neg\alpha \iff T_i \nvdash \alpha$$

From completeness, the other properties follow at once. For instance:

Lemma 2.0.18. [T_i is Prime] *For every index I and $i \subseteq I$,*
$$T_i \vdash \alpha \vee \beta \iff T_i \vdash \alpha \text{ or } T_i \vdash \beta$$

Proof. We have the $\Leftarrow$ direction as a consequence of the rule of disjunction introduction. For the $\Rightarrow$ direction, we argue indirectly. Suppose that $T_i \nvdash \alpha$ and also that $T_i \nvdash \beta$. It follows by completeness that $T_i \vdash \neg\alpha$ and $T_i \vdash \neg\beta$. But then $T_i \vdash (\neg\alpha \wedge \neg\beta)$ which is to say that $T_i \vdash \neg(\alpha \vee \beta)$. By consistency then, $T_i \nvdash \alpha \vee \beta$. □

Lemma 2.0.19. [T_i is Implicative] *For every index I and $i \subseteq I$,*
$$T_i \vdash \beta \supset \gamma \iff T_i \vdash \beta \Rightarrow T_i \vdash \gamma$$

Proof. The proof is left as an exercise. □

2.1 Metalogic

The central metalogical result for classical logic connects the proof theory with the semantics. It will turn out that we can use the results of the last section to, in effect, *re-construct* the central semantic idea, that of an assignment, 'inside' our proof theory. We start with:

Theorem 2.1.1 (Correspondence Theorem for *CSL*). *For every index I and $i \subseteq I$ and for every formula α of SL_I,*
$$\models_{v_i} \alpha \iff T_i \vdash \alpha$$

Proof. This follows from the uniqueness of truth-functional extensions together with the observation that $T_i \vdash$ *is* a truth-functional extension of v_i. □

What we need to do now is to connect our syntactical reconstruction of the semantics with the relation between provability and semantic entailment. The latter is defined for arbitrary pairs $\langle \Gamma, \alpha \rangle$ using the notion of truth relative to to an assignment v_i, in the familiar way. The former also defines a relation for arbitrary pairs, but our syntactical equivalent of truth relative to v_i is $T_i \vdash$, where T_i is not at all arbitrary.

There must be some way to connect the theories T_i with arbitrary sets of formulas of SL_I.

An obvious place to start is with the question of whether we can embed an arbitrary (consistent) set of formulas of SL_I into some T_i. To carry out this *extension* we need to be able to find a 'compatible' diagram. The following construction[3] takes care of that. We first define:

Definition 2.1.2. Let Γ be an arbitrary consistent set of formulas of SL_I and suppose all the members of I have been placed in an 'urn' (a familiar thought experiment from probability and statistics). We can now build up a sequence of sets: $\Sigma_0, \Sigma_1, \ldots$, in the following way

$$\Sigma_0 = \Gamma$$

$\vdots$

$$\Sigma_k = \begin{cases} \Sigma_{k-1} \cup \{\alpha_k\} & \text{if this is consistent,} \\ \Sigma_{k-1} \cup \{\neg\alpha_k\} & \text{otherwise.} \end{cases}$$

$\vdots$

---

[3]This construction was suggested by Luke Fraser.

In this construction α_k is the kth member of I which is drawn from the urn. After the kth stage, that atomic sentence is not returned to the urn. The sequence continues until the urn is empty.

Σ^+ is defined to be the union of all the stages, or alternatively, if the sequence is finite, the last member.

$$i_\Gamma = \{\alpha \in I \,|\, \alpha \in \Sigma^+\}$$

It is important to notice here that if $\beta \in I$ does not belong to i_Γ, it must be the case that $\Sigma^+, \beta \vdash \perp$ and hence, by [¬I] $\Sigma^+ \vdash \neg\beta$. This means that when we form the diagram of i_Γ we take the union of two sets: i_Γ which is consistent with Γ by definition, and $\{\neg\beta \,|\, \beta \in I \,\&\, \beta \notin i_\Gamma\}$, all the members of which are proved by $\Gamma \cup i_\Gamma$.

Lemma 2.1.3. $\Gamma \cup \mathbb{D}_{i_\Gamma} \nvdash \perp$

Proof. Suppose, for reductio, that the set is inconsistent after all.

Then there must be n and m such that

$$\Gamma, \alpha_1, \ldots, \alpha_n, \neg\beta_1, \ldots, \neg\beta_m \vdash \perp$$

where the α formulas are from i_Γ and the $\neg\beta$ formulas are all from the other half of $\mathbb{D}_{i_\Gamma}$.

But $\Gamma, \alpha_1, \ldots, \alpha_n \vdash \neg\beta_k$ for $1 \le k \le m$, as noted above.

Now an n-fold application of the rule [T] gives us the result

$\Gamma, \alpha_1, \ldots, \alpha_n \vdash \perp$, which is impossible by the definition of i_Γ.

$\square$

We make a stylistic variation to avoid double subscripting

Definition 2.1.4. $T_\Gamma = \mathbb{C}_\vdash(\mathbb{D}_{i_\Gamma})$

We would like to show now that $\Gamma \subseteq T_\Gamma$. But to do that we need to appeal to a general property of the theories T_i. That property is:

The property **max**, of *maximality* is defined

Definition 2.1.5. $\mathbf{max}(\Delta) \iff [\alpha \notin \Delta \implies \Delta, \alpha \vdash \bot]$

Lemma 2.1.6. *For every index I and $i \subseteq I$* $\mathbf{max}(T_i)$

Proof. The lemma is an obvious consequence of the completeness property of the theories T_i. $\qquad \square$

With this behind us we can show that T_Γ contains Γ.

Lemma 2.1.7 ((Little) Lindenbaum Lemma). *For every index I, every consistent set Γ, of formulas of SL_I can be extended to T_i for some $i \subseteq I$.*

Proof. We should notice first that

> $T_\Gamma \cup \Gamma \nvdash \bot$ else, by an application of [T], Γ would be inconsistent with $\mathbb{D}_{i_\Gamma}$, which we know to be impossible from lemma 2.1.3.

> But we know from lemma 2.1.6 that $\mathbf{max}(T_\Gamma)$ so that if any member of Γ were not a member of T_Γ, $T_\Gamma \cup \Gamma \vdash \bot$.

> So every member of Γ must be a member of T_Γ, which is to say

> $\Gamma \subseteq T_\Gamma$

$\qquad \square$

2.2 Overview of the Main Result

In the central investigation of this chapter we shall take up the question of the relationship between four propositions. In order to state these more economically, we introduce some notation.

$\Gamma \vdash^i \alpha$ abbreviates $T_i \vdash \Gamma \implies T_i \vdash \alpha$ for every index i and $i \subseteq I$.

$\Gamma \vDash^i \alpha$ abbreviates $\vDash_{v_i} \Gamma \implies \vDash_{v_i} \alpha$ for every index I and $i \subseteq I$.

We shall take the core result for the metalogic of CSL to be the demonstration that certain assertions are all equivalent. For ease of presentation, the four assertions in question are laid out in the *Equivalence Diagram for CSL*.

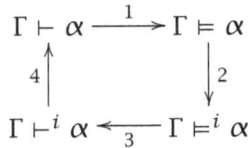

$$\begin{array}{ccc}
\Gamma \vdash \alpha & \xrightarrow{\ 1\ } & \Gamma \vDash \alpha \\[2pt]
{\scriptstyle 4}\uparrow & & \downarrow{\scriptstyle 2} \\[2pt]
\Gamma \vdash^i \alpha & \xleftarrow{\ 3\ } & \Gamma \vDash^i \alpha
\end{array}$$

Figure 2.1: The Equivalence Diagram for CSL

If each of the arrows in this picture represents an implication relation ($\implies$), then obviously all the four 'corners' are equivalent. What we might call the standard way of presenting the metalogic of CLS is a bit like that. We shall present some comments on the matter later in this section and the next.

Our approach will be rather different. We notice that the arrow labeled 2 stands for $\iff$ in virtue of the fact that entailment is defined to be the relation $\vDash^i$.

It also seems that the arrow 3 likewise represents a metalanguage biconditional as a consequence of the correspondence theorem. We shall prove this.

Finally, the arrow 4 clearly holds from top to bottom
by appeal to monotonicity. We shall show that the other
direction holds as well, as a consequence of the so-called
Little Lindenbaum Lemma.

But if any three arrows in the diagram represent the $\iff$
relation, then so must the forth (by diagram chasing). Here
are the bits laid out in a more official-looking form.

Theorem 2.2.1 (Equivalence Theorem for *CSL*). *The following are all equivalent to one another:*

[truth-preservation] $\Gamma \vDash^i \alpha$
[proof-preservation]$\Gamma \vdash^i \alpha$
[provability] $\Gamma \vdash \alpha$
[entailment] $\Gamma \vDash \alpha$

Proof. The result follows from the following two results
and the fact that entailment is defined as $\vDash^i$.

$\square$

Theorem 2.2.2 (Proof-Preservation Theorem for *CSL*). *For
every index I, $i \subseteq I$, and pair Γ, α*

$$\Gamma \vdash \alpha \iff \Gamma \vdash^i \alpha$$

Proof. For the left to right direction ($\Longrightarrow$), since the T_i are
all theories, if any should prove all the members of Γ, they
must also contain Γ as a subset. Thus [M] shows that whatever Γ proves, the theories which contain Γ must likewise
prove. For the right-to-left direction ($\Longleftarrow$) we shall show
that when $\Gamma \nvdash \alpha$ there will be at least one T_i which satisfies the condition of the theorem such that $T_i \vdash \neg\alpha$ (which
obviously implies that $T_i \nvdash \alpha$). Consider the set $\Gamma \cup \{\neg\alpha\}$.
This must be consistent or else $\Gamma \vdash \alpha$ by [$\neg$E], contrary to

the hypothesis that $\Gamma \nvdash \alpha$. But if the set is consistent we know from the Little Lindenbaum Lemma that there is a T_i, namely T_Γ which contains Γ and which proves $\neg\alpha$). Thus, by indirect proof, if $\Gamma \vdash^i \alpha$ then $\Gamma \vdash \alpha$, which is just what we wanted. □

Theorem 2.2.3 (Equivalence of preservation for CSL). *For every index I, $i \subseteq I$, and pair Γ, α*

$$\Gamma \vdash^i \alpha \iff \Gamma \vDash^i \alpha$$

Proof. Assume that $\Gamma \vdash^i \alpha$. Hence by definition of that relation, this will hold if and only if for every $i \subseteq I$, if $T_i \vdash \Gamma$ then $T_i \vdash \alpha$. But from the Correspondence Theorem for CSL (Theorem 2.1.1) this can hold if and only if $\vDash_{v_i} \Gamma$ implies $\vDash_{v_i} \alpha$ for all $i \subseteq I$. □

Part One:
Modal and Many-Valued Logics

Three

Introduction to Modal Logic

3.1 Introduction and Brief History

Modal logic is supposed to be the logic of necessity and possibility. Having said this, one should realize that one hasn't said very much, or at least very much that would excite universal approval and agreement. Historically, modal logic begins with the logical work of Aristotle who, so it is claimed, used 'necessarily' sometimes as a synonym for 'deductively' and sometimes as a logical word in its own right. As an example of the former, Aristotle will claim that an inference with premises $P_1, \ldots, P_n$ and conclusion C is valid by saying that if P_1, and ... and P_n, then *necessarily C* (emphasis added). We shall have reason to inquire below if such usage really is mere synonymy.

One can also find, in various bits of the organon, a fragmentary account of modal syllogistic. Aristotle's treatment of modality seems to some contemporary authors to be not entirely adequate. Some have argued, for example, that he was never able to free himself of certain equivocations in the meanings of the key modal terms 'necessarily' and 'possibly.' Historians of logic now seem to be generally agreed that Aristotle's logical critics and rivals of the (later) Hellenistic period presented a better account of modality. The approach favored during that period tended to be a temporal one in which possibility and necessity are to be explained in terms of sometimes and always. This analysis was very influential in the ancient world, particularly in connection with the so-called master argument[1] of Diodorus.

Some form of the temporal interpretation persisted without much challenge until the highest point of medieval logic was reached in the fourteenth century. At that time it was argued by Duns Scotus that temporal considerations alone are inadequate for the analysis of necessity. The context for this argument was the famous debate between Ockham and Scotus on predestination and in this debate we find Scotus claiming that as well as moments of time, a proper understanding of modal terminology requires reference to 'moments of nature.' In saying this Scotus can be seen as anticipating many of the recent developments and for this reason it is tempting to call the contemporary approach to modal logic 'Scotian.'

Recent work in modal logic begins at the end of the nineteenth century with the American logician and philosopher C. S. Pierce, and the English mathematician Hugh MacColl.[2] Pierce's work is well-known, although his logical work less so. His modal logic occurs in the system of *gamma graphs*, and takes as the primitive modal concept, impossibility. The exposition is hampered by a notation most suitable to blackboards and slates (and in fact it seems to have been devised to that end) so that interest in this style of logic was bound to decline with the fall in the price of paper.

When people know anything at all of MacColl, it is usually that he was on the losing end of a debate with Bertrand

---

[1]Logicians, following A.N. Prior, seem to favor this name for the argument, while historians of Hellenistic philosophy are just as likely to call it the 'ruling argument.'

[2]See (MacColl, 1903, 1906).

Russell at the turn of the century. Russell's contention in this debate was that MacColl's interest in modal functions betrays a failure to understand the concept of a propositional function (i.e. what we would now call an open sentence). This amounts to a failure to grasp the distinction between propositional logic and quantification theory. A more dispassionate appraisal of MacColl's work might well conclude that he understood the difference very well though he was not inclined to classify quantification theory as logic, but rather as a less general science.

It is hard not to see the Russell-MacColl encounter as a pivotal event in the recent history of modal logic. Although Russell felt himself free to change his mind on any subject whatever (which freedom he exercised frequently) he never gave up his hard line on modality. Early in his famous Lectures on Logical Atomism, for example, we find him claiming that most philosophical talk about possibility and necessity is simply a ham-fisted attempt to deploy concepts better represented by existential and universal quantification. When the center of formal logic shifted from England and the Continent to the United States, many of Russell's views on the nature and purpose of logic fell out of fashion but the new power structure maintained the Russellian line on the logical analysis of modality. In fact this line was developed along two distinct branches.

One branch, for a time the most significant, we might call mathematical. Among the most powerful figures in formal logic from the 1920's to virtually the present day were mathematicians whose interest in logic was bound up in one or more of the foundational programs. This group, led by Weyl and others, actively discouraged research on modal logic on the grounds that no formal account of the modal words is required by the analysis of mathematical reasoning. Modal logic is thus a waste of valuable (and scarce) resources which would be more productively employed in standard proof-theory, recursive function theory, and the like.

In those halcyon days people were a lot more excited about foundational studies than they are today. Given that most of the subscribers to this mathematical denunciation of modal logic were committed to programs which they felt to be enormously worthwhile, even vital, to the whole edifice of science, their motivation is understandable. But, it must be admitted, there is little else to be said for such a view. It is simply false that the formal analysis of necessity engenders no mathematically interesting questions and false also that modal logic can make no contribution to our understanding of the formalization of mathematics.

The other branch is composed of those with philosophical objections to the doing of modal logic. In this case the motivation is not so clear. One might have hoped that since philosophers were largely responsible for the rebirth of modal logic in the twentieth century, other philosophers would rally to the standard once the mathematicians began to exercise their malign influence. Unfortunately these hopes would have been dashed. Instead, a group arose, with W.V.O. Quine in the vanguard, to propose a nest of reasons for abandoning modal research forthwith.

The weight of all this disapproval was most assuredly felt. Throughout the 1930s, 1940s and much of the 1950s, modal logic became a kind of banned science. Young researchers soon got the message that although everyone could have a hobby, one's serious work–the work that one intends for publication, should be in the mainstream. It would be an interesting and important project in the history of recent logic to gauge the effect of this suppression movement more precisely.

Twentieth century modal logic begins in earnest in the second decade of the 20th Century both on the Continent and, under the previously mentioned cloud, in the United

States. Continental modal logic was centered on the Polish school led by Łukasiewicz, with the German philosopher and logician Oskar Becker also playing a crucial role. In the United States, C.I. Lewis of Harvard[3] and (a decade or two later) H.B Smith[4] of the University of Pennsylvania, together with their students, were the ones to swim against the tide.

The Polish school has been documented in a number of places and certainly it would be hard to overestimate its contribution to logic. This also is true for modal logic, although in that instance, the contribution is somewhat roundabout. Łukasiewicz himself was primarily interested in many-valued logic, and modal considerations entered through his attempts to interpret the "non-classical" values. So in the first instance, he considered "possible" as the meaning of the third truth-value in his three-valued system. Later in life, he switched to a four-valued logic as the correct logic of possibility. Both projects had the drawback that they treated modal terms as being truth-functional, and thus flew in the face of everyone else's most cherished intuitions, according to which if we know the truth-value of α, it doesn't follow that we know the truth-value of necessarily-α or of possibly-α.

In the United States, both Lewis and Smith were interested in a binary modal connective, that they called strict implication, and implication respectively. Lewis thought of himself as repairing the *Principia Mathematica* account of implication, which had come to be called *material implication*, while Smith began from scratch (as he saw it). There was little contact between the two schools, though both were familiar with the work of the Continental schools (especially Becker). The Lewis approach starts with noticing

---

[3] See (Lewis, 1913, 1914b,a, 1918b), (note that the second edition of *Survey* does not contain the final chapter on strict implication).

[4] See (Churchman, 1942) and (Smith, 1934)

that the following 'laws of thought:'

$$\alpha \supset (\beta \supset \alpha)$$
$$\neg\alpha \supset (\alpha \supset \beta)$$
$$(\alpha \supset \beta) \vee (\beta \supset \alpha)$$

don't seem to be correct when we read the "$\supset$" as "implies," since they say that a true sentence is implied by every sentence, a false sentence implies every sentence and, in every pair of sentences, one implies the other. These are some others had come to be called *paradoxes of material implication.*

To flesh this out a bit, Lewis provides some informal semantics for the notion of "implies" on which none of the above are laws of thought:

'α strictly implies β' is true if and only if β is deducible from α.

For it is clear that one cannot deduce an arbitrary sentence from an arbitrary false sentence (with no other information). Neither can one (invariably) construct a deduction from an arbitrary sentence to an arbitrary true sentence. And finally, there are plenty of pairs of sentences for which no deduction can be constructed in either direction.

Possibility and necessity enter as an adjunct to the account of this strict conditional. We can of course (and Lewis did) just write down a bunch of principles which govern this new conditionality but, to aid the neophyte, we can also localize the source of the above paradoxes of material implication in the fact that the conditional in question can be defined by:

Definition 3.1.1. '$\alpha \supset \beta$' for '$\neg(\alpha \wedge \neg\beta)$'

---

while genuine (i.e. strict) implication must mean more than the falsehood of true antecedent and false consequent— it must mean the *impossibility* of that combination. Using '→' to represent the strict conditional, and '◊' to represent possibility, we would write this:

Definition 3.1.2. '$\alpha \to \beta$' for '$\neg \Diamond (\alpha \wedge \neg \beta)$'

While Lewis was working on his deducibility interpretation and trying to discover *the* system of strict implication (there were three that he thought of as contenders at one time or another, and others that he thought were worthy of study), H.B. Smith was working on a rather different semantic approach. For Smith, the correct truth-condition for implication is:

'α implies β' is true if and only if 'α' implies 'β.'

Indeed this obviously *is* correct, and more informative than one might at first expect. For Smith the truth-condition has these consequences:

'$\alpha \to \alpha$' must be a 'law of thought'

'→' is not a truth-functional operator

In turn these spawn many derived principles. For example it was clear to Smith that one of the (many) false doctrines associated with classical logic was the view that there are only two propositions (the true and the false). Genuine logic, Smith felt, must acknowledge infinitely many propositions, and genuine implication would do so by distinguishing (in the first instance) between '$\alpha \to \perp$' and '$\neg \alpha$' (notice that by principles of classical reasoning, no such distinction can be made when we replace the strict conditional with the material one: '$\supset$'). The former represents the impossibility of α while the latter is the simple unvarnished falsehood of α. So for Smith, possibility is defined in terms of implication, while for Lewis, it's the other way about. Although of course for both, implication is the central concern with the unary modal operators taking a distant second place in their hearts.

This preoccupation continued into the 1930's when the German philosopher Becker single-handedly changed the focus of research in modal logic. In his paper (Becker, 1930), he studied a number of different logics which were mainly distinguished by their treatment of the modal operators, especially in combination with each other. Since that time, implication has occupied a smaller and smaller portion of the attention of philosophical logicians, at least in connection with modal logic. This disregard of what Lewis and Smith would have regarded as the whole point of modal logic, reached an apex (or perhaps nadir) in 1957 when E.J. Lemmon in (Lemmon, 1957) published a new formalization of the various Lewis systems, in which no mention at all of strict implication is made. Most contemporary presentations of the subject now follow Lemmon.

It turns out that concentrating on the unary modal notions allows one to think of the whole enterprise of modal logic as constructing a plausible extension of classical logic rather than fixing it. This in turn facilitates the asking of the right kinds of questions. For example we can ask: Given that our account of the classical operators is thus-and-so, what kind of account of the modal operators best fits into this framework? The influence of the Polish school reasserts itself at this point when in 1951 Tarski, the most prominent of Łukasiewicz' students, together with his doctoral student Jónson, published (Tarski and Jónsson, 1951), which answers this question. Even though this work is couched in the terminology of algebra it is astonishing that it passed unremarked since it anticipates virtually every significant aspect of the 'possible-worlds semantics' which so galvanized philosophical logic in the 1960's and 1970's.

3.2 An Account of the Necessary

We shall follow the post-Becker tradition in pursuing necessity and possibility in their own right rather than as derivatives from some more central modal notion. But we do not adopt this stance out of contempt for the Lewis-Smith tradition; indeed we feel that tradition respects certain very important intuitions. As it will turn out, our formalization of modal logic owes a recognizable debt to the 'implicationists'.

The problem with necessity is that there seems to be rather a lot of different kinds of it about. Although we often use modal words like 'necessary' and 'possible,' a little reflection shows that we use them in a variety of contexts relative to which the meanings of the terms display a similar variety. In spite of this, there is a rough and ready taxonomy on which we may classify at least some of the species of necessity.

The traditional categories are logical necessity, mathematical necessity, and, physical necessity. These are supposed to be ordered by inclusion in the sense that the smallest set is the set of logically necessary truths, which is properly included in the set of mathematically necessary truths which is, in its turn, properly included in the set of physically necessary truths. There are other categories too: moral necessity and psychological necessity to name just a couple. But when we get beyond the 'big three' our intuitions concerning orderings amongst the categories drop off rather steeply.

Keeping these things in mind, let us have a go at what seems to be the base class—logical necessity. Not only is this a more appropriate notion for us as logicians to study, many authors feel that other notions of necessity are best seen as *derived* from logical necessity. So some sentence α is *physically* necessary would mean, on such a view, that a conditional of some sort: $L \rightarrow \alpha$, is logically necessary, where L represents the conjunction of the laws of physics.

The Received View

The most influential view on the nature of logical necessity would have it that the latter is no more and no less than truth, in all possible worlds. That a host of difficulties follow in its train, seems not to worry those who have received this account, but it will worry us.

Let us consider some of these difficulties.

> You say that necessary truth is truth in all possible worlds?
> Yes, just as Leibniz tells us.
> He certainly tells us something like that, but it isn't the only thing he tells us.
> Well, I'm not claiming that the contemporary account is anything more than *inspired* by the Leibniz dictum.
> But aren't you worried that on this so-called dictum there won't be any necessary truths?
> No, of course not, we can find plenty of examples.
> Really? Would you care to offer one?
> Certainly $\alpha \supset \alpha$ is necessarily true. It is perhaps the clearest example.
> Aha. Well, I'm not sure how to tell you this, but I have a possible world in my back pocket, and in that world $\alpha \supset \alpha$ is not true. So I guess it isn't necessary after all, eh?
> *Au contraire*! Your claim to have on hand a possible world like that is self-defeating. Any world in which $\alpha \supset \alpha$ fails, also fails to be a (logically) pos-

sible world, and thus cannot be a counter-example to the necessary truth in question.

That's a bit brisk, isn't it? Do you really want to assert that my world fails to be possible?

I most certainly do want to assert that, and so does Leibniz.

Leaving aside your friend for the moment, what you appeal to when you rule on the admissibility of my world is some account of possibility.

Yes, I suppose that I do. At least I have an account of what features a world must enjoy in order to count as a logically possible world.

But if you *already* have a theory of logical possibility, you must *ipso facto* have a theory of logical necessity. In that case, you owe us an account of that theory.

No problem in doing that. To paraphrase Leibnitz again, whatever follows from the law of non-contradiction is necessary and if the negation of a proposition doesn't follow from that law, then it is possible.

And, I presume you want to say that my world cannot be logically possible since the negation of $\alpha \supset \alpha$ holds in it, but the negation of that negation follows from the law of non-contradiction?

Precisely, and so your world isn't possible since in it, a proposition holds, the negation of which follows from the law. Where's the grief?

Leaving aside your assuming that since $\alpha \supset \alpha$ doesn't hold in my world, its negation does, which is a lot to leave aside, can there be anything, any proposition at all, which is necessarily true and not logically true?

Hmmm, well I don't see why not.

Neither did Leibnitz but then he used the principle of sufficient reason as well as the law of non-contradiction in his account of necessity. You don't.

What difference does that make?

Just this: If some proposition is not logically true, then there must be at least one possible world, on your account, in which that proposition is false. Otherwise, it would follow from the law of non-contradiction, and hence be necessary.

Oh well, say you're right—so what?

So you don't really have an account of necessary truth at all, merely an account of logical truth under a different name. But we already know about logical truth and surely we don't need another name for it.

Although it might not be apparent at first glance, this criticism of the received view is closely related to one produced by Quine in (Quine, 1953).

An Alternative

But if it isn't truth in all possible worlds, what *is* logical necessity? What else could it possibly be but deduction, just as Aristotle says? Of course this needs to be amplified and clarified. We say that *sentences* are the objects which are necessary; In other words, we aim to give an account of *necessary truth.* So which sentences are the ones which we would say, intuitively, are necessary as a matter of logic? Surely it's *conclusions* which best fit this description.

More particularly, the conclusions of *deductions* fall into this category, if any sentences do. Although, if we think for a bit, we shall discover a problem with those sentences too. Just imagine a case in which we find the conclusion of a deduction repugnant, for whatever reason. Are we really stuck with it no matter what we do? Not as logic is usually understood. For if we find the conclusion distasteful enough, it is usually open to us to reject one or more of the premises from which it was deduced. In fact this is a recognized technique for getting somebody to give up allegiance to some premise set—just find some unpleasant enough conclusion, to which one can point regretfully.

To fix this, necessary truths need to be the conclusions of deductions from premises to which we are *committed*, which is to say that we can't (or won't) take any of them back. Notice that there must be at least one kind of case in which we have that kind of commitment i.e. the case of deductions in which the premises are themselves necessary. It turns out that Aristotle has a term for such deductions: they are called *demonstrations*. So that what this account comes down to may be put into the form of the slogan:

> *The conclusion of every demonstration is a necessary truth.*

We now require two things, a truth condition and the rules of proof. Both it turns out, flow from the Aristotelian insight that necessity resides in the connection between the premises and the conclusion of a deduction.

3.3 Proof Theory

We shall use the symbol $\square$ as the object language representation of logical necessity. Our Aristotelian slogan translates very directly into this extended vocabulary, although it doesn't lead in any obvious way to a pair of rules (i.e. to an introduction rule and an elimination rule for $\square$). This much is clear: If $\Gamma \vdash \alpha$, then if all the members of Γ are necessary, then so must α be necessary. This is because, if the members of Γ are necessary then they must be sentences to which we are committed.

We get a single rule; one which introduces the square on both sides of the turnstile at once (in formulating this rule we use the 'square brackets' notation introduced in the first chapter):

$$[R\square]\ \Gamma \vdash P \ \Rightarrow\ \square[\Gamma] \vdash \square P$$

We shall say, in accord with custom, that our fundamental modal rule axiomatizes *normal* modal logic—assuming that it is used on top of the usual classical rules for sentential logic.

It must be admitted that this rule is not part of the standard proof-theory of normal modal logic even though it springs directly from our motivation. There are actually two standard presentations: an earlier one and a later one. The earlier one can be found in the work of Gődel (Gődel, 1933), Lemmon (Lemmon, 1957), Kripke (Kripke, 1963), and Hughes and Cresswell (Cresswell and Hughes, 1968), and is still the most prevalent. In this we formalize modal logic by adding a new law of thought to the classical stock of such, and adding an additional rule under which the class is required to be closed.

$$[K']\ \square(\alpha \supset \beta) \supset (\square\alpha \supset \square\beta)$$
$$[RN]\ \vdash \alpha \ \Rightarrow\ \vdash \square\alpha$$

The later presentation is due primarily to Segerberg.[5] While it is also in the laws of thought tradition, it has the advantage of recognizing that the law [K'] represents an amalgam of two quite different principles. These are split

---

[5](Segerberg, 1971)

up into a law and another rule:

$$[K] \; (\Box\alpha \land \Box\beta) \supset \Box(\alpha \land \beta)$$
$$[RM] \; \vdash \alpha \supset \beta \; \Rightarrow \; \Box\alpha \supset \Box\beta$$
$$[RN] \; \vdash \alpha \; \Rightarrow \; \vdash \Box\alpha$$

The names we assign to these principles are not arbitrary. Segerberg uses the [K] in honor of Saul Kripke, and the other tradition uses the same letter which we have changed to [K'] to avoid ambiguity. We use the name [RM] to suggest 'rule of monotonicity,' where Segerberg uses [RR] for the same principle which he calls the 'rule of regularity.' We use [RN] for the 'rule of normality' but the majority refer to is as the 'rule of necessitation' instead.

So under the Segerberg proof-theory, the class of laws of thought is required to contain every instance of [K] and to be closed under both [RN] and [RM] as well as the classical rules. With a little ingenuity, it is possible to show that all three presentations are in fact equivalent; that within any one, the principles of any of the others may be derived. This is, most emphatically, not to say that all three are 'really the same.' The advantage of Segerberg's formalization over the earlier one has already been canvassed. But both the standard presentations have the demerit of being squarely in the laws of thought tradition.

This is awkward because, as we have urged, necessity is not about the laws of thought, at least in the first instance. On the classical picture, the laws must be necessary since they are (by definition) exactly the sentences that follow from the empty set of premises. Of course since the empty set of premises contains no premises, we are committed to all of them).

The smallest normal modal logic, or alternatively, the intersection of all of them, we shall refer to by means of K. When it becomes necessary to do so, we shall subscript our 'turnstile' symbol with a K, in the manner of '$\vdash_K$.'

3.4   Model Theory

When it comes to defining entailment for modal logic, we see at once that we cannot use the classical picture as is. Our proto-truth-condition requires that the truth-value of $\Box \alpha$ depends upon more than the truth-value of α, and in the classical (also called the truth-functional) picture, the truth-value of α is all we have.

What we need is some way of saying that α is a consequence of the set of sentences to which we are committed. This requires first that we have a way of representing different 'situations' or 'contexts' with respect to which our commitments to certain sentences are specified. This is actually pretty easy—what we need is a set of these objects, let's call it $\mathbb{U}$ (for universe perhaps). The next part isn't quite so easy, but knowing roughly what we want in the way of a truth-condition, and adopting the classical theory of inference, (almost) all that we need to do, is make the truth of sentences relative to the members of $\mathbb{U}$. So the 'contexts of commitment,' or whatever, are going to have to do double duty as the objects with respect to which sentences take on truth values as well.

Perhaps in the hope of helping $\mathbb{U}$ bear up under this crushing responsibility, some have taken to the bestowing of grandiloquent titles. Members of $\mathbb{U}$ are not to be called 'contexts,' we are enjoined, but rather *possible worlds*.

Alas, a sanitation engineer is usually no better at collecting garbage than a garbage collector. Indeed, the main difference may be that the engineer will require wages commensurate with the title. In like manner have the members of $\mathbb{U}$ gotten above themselves, becoming objects of veneration in some quarters and generally interfering with clear thinking about matters modal. In an effort to steam against this tide, we shall refer to them as points.

Making truth relative to points interferes hardly at all

with the truth-conditions for the classical connectives. All the classically compounded sentences will be evaluated as usual, save only that such evaluation will now be relative to points. But the truth-condition for sentences beginning with square will require another bit of elaboration on our semantic structure, which thus far consists of a naked set $\mathbb{U}$. Recall that (informally) we want to say that α is (logically) necessarily true (relative to a point u, say) if and only if α is a consequence of the set of sentences to which we are committed at u. All we need is some way of picking out, for each point u, the set of points v, such that every sentence to which we are committed at u, is true at v.

Since we have decided to let sentences be true or false relative to points, there is no barrier to simply producing a function or relation which does this picking out. Now it's clear that if α is true at every such 'picked out' point, this amounts to saying that α is entailed (classically) by the set of our commitments at u. Let us now gather all this lore together and systematize it. Our basic semantic structure consists of a (non-empty) set $\mathbb{U}$, together with a binary relation R, defined on $\mathbb{U}$. A pair of this sort will be called a *frame*, and we shall use $\mathcal{F}$, $\mathcal{F}_1$, etc. to refer to such.

Where $\mathcal{F} = (\mathbb{U}, R)$ is a frame, $\mathbb{U}$ will be called the *underlying set* of $\mathcal{F}$, and R the *underlying relation* or, more often, the *frame relation*. In order to evaluate sentences, we require something akin to the classical notion of an assignment; something which tells us the truth values of all the atomic sentences. All these tales will be now be relative to the points of the underlying set of some frame. To this end we employ the notion of a *valuation*, represented by V, V_1, etc., which is a function from atomic-sentence, point pairs to the set $\{0, 1\}$. When $V(\alpha, u) = 1$, we interpret this informally as 'The atomic sentence α is true relative to (or at) the point u.'

A pair (or triple really) consisting of a frame together

with a valuation is called a *model*. Models will be repre-
sented by means of $\mathcal{M}$, $\mathcal{M}_1$, etc. and when $\mathcal{M} = (\mathcal{F}, V)$ is
a model, $\mathcal{F}$ is called the *underlying frame*. We shall some-
times use the notation $\mathcal{F}(\mathcal{M})$ to indicate the underlying
frame of $\mathcal{M}$. It is really relative to models that we define
truth. To be more specific we define the predicate 'α is
true at the point u in the model $\mathcal{M}$,' represented by the
notation: $\mathcal{M}, u \vDash \alpha$. The basis clause of our recursive definition is as we expect:

$$\mathcal{M}, u \vDash \alpha \iff V(\alpha, u) = 1, \text{ if } \alpha \in \mathbf{At}$$

while the recursion clauses go as promised for the
classical connectives:

$$[\wedge] \; \mathcal{M}, u \vDash \alpha \wedge \beta \iff (\mathcal{M}, u \vDash \alpha \,\&\, \mathcal{M}, u \vDash \beta$$
$$[\vee] \; \mathcal{M}, u \vDash \alpha \vee \beta \iff (\mathcal{M}, u \vDash \alpha \text{ or } \mathcal{M}, u \vDash \beta)$$
$$[\supset] \; \mathcal{M}, u \vDash \alpha \supset \beta \iff (\mathcal{M}, u \vDash \alpha \implies \mathcal{M}, u \vDash \beta)$$
$$[\neg] \; \mathcal{M}, u \vDash \neg\alpha \iff \mathcal{M}, u \nvDash \alpha)$$

For the modal connective we follow exactly our earlier,
informal account:

$$[\square] \; \mathcal{M}, u \vDash \square\alpha \iff (\forall v)(Ruv \implies \mathcal{M}, v \vDash \alpha)$$

When things were simple and classical we had but a single class of objects to worry about—the class of assignments. In the current setup, we have two sorts of objects:
models and frames. What we have now is a definition of
truth at a point u, in a model $\mathcal{M}$. What we want is a definition of entailment. It occurs to us first is to define

Definition 3.4.1. $\Gamma \models^{\mathcal{M}} \alpha$ if and only if, if all the members of Γ are true at any point of $\mathcal{M}$, then so is α true at that point.

We can define entailment *simpliciter* to hold when the latter relation holds for every $\mathcal{M}$, or more generally, we shall define entailment relative to a class C of models:

Definition 3.4.2. $\Gamma \models \alpha[C]$ if and only if $\Gamma \models^{\mathcal{M}} \alpha$ for every $\mathcal{M}$ in the class (of models) C.

This is definitely a notion of entailment, but it isn't the only one we can construct. In particular, we can also define entailment with respect to frames rather than models:

Definition 3.4.3. $\Gamma \models^{\mathcal{F}} \alpha$ if and only if $\Gamma \models^{\mathcal{M}} \alpha$ for every $\mathcal{M}$ such that $\mathcal{F}(\mathcal{M}) = \mathcal{F}$.

Here again we can define entailment 'in a class of frames C,' by quantifying away the $\mathcal{F}$ in the last definition.

Definition 3.4.4. '$\Gamma \models \alpha[C]$' for '$(\forall \mathcal{M})[\mathcal{F}(\mathcal{M}) \in C \implies (\mathcal{M}, u \models \Gamma \implies \mathcal{M}, u \models \alpha)]$'

This is all a bit confusing, but it's important to realize that we haven't defined distinct notions of entailment in any important sense. If α is entailed by Γ in the frame $\mathcal{F}$, this will amount to being entailed by Γ in the class of models defined over that frame. Similarly being entailed by Γ relative to a class of frames is obviously equivalent to being entailed by Γ relative to the class of all models defined over each member of that class of frames. The reason for the 'frame theoretic' definitions, is so that we can connect the model theory of modal logic with the model theory of *elementary logic*, i.e. first-order quantificational logic. There will be such a connection since a frame (in our sense) is what in elementary logic is called a model (of the first-order theory of one binary relation).[6]

There is a somewhat different style of semantics when we have some definite *logic* in mind.

Definition 3.4.5. $\mathcal{M}$ is a model *for* the logic L if and only if, $\Gamma \vdash_L \alpha \implies \Gamma \vDash^{\mathcal{M}} \alpha$.

And this in turn gives us an alternative way to define semantic entailment:

Definition 3.4.6. $\Gamma \vDash_L \alpha \iff$ if $\mathcal{M}$ is a model for L, then $\Gamma \vDash^{\mathcal{M}} \alpha$

Given our definition of the 'basic' normal modal logic K, it is easy to see that:

Proposition 3.4.7. *Every model is a model for K.*

3.5   Metatheory of Modal Logic

We use the same strategy in dealing with metalogical issues now, as we did before. The idea is to reconstruct our semantics inside our proof theory. Previously we needed only get ourselves a syntactic equivalent of a truth-value assignment, but now our semantics has become more complex. Our class of maximal theories $\mathbb{T}_i$, might conceivably be pressed into service as points, but this still leaves us

---

[6]In this connection see the important paper (Fine, 1975).

looking for the equivalent of the frame relation R. We are also under a cloud of doubt as regards whether or not our existing notion of a maximal theory will be able to stand up under a heavier load. We need to be able to appeal (as we did earlier) to the fact that such theories satisfy proof-conditions which exactly parallel the recursion clauses of the definition of truth (i.e. the truth-conditions).

Having expanded our language we now have one extra truth-condition to worry about: the condition for $\Box$. It turns out that the two issues are intertwined: by a judicious choice of the relation we can avoid the need for further fixing. Our proof theory has been expanded from the classical, and hence what we mean by a theory has changed accordingly. We shall use a subscript to show which notion of theoryhood is at issue in the manner of: $\mathbb{T}_L^+$, which denotes the class of L fixed theories. Until further notice, L will be a normal modal logic. Often, when it is clear from the context which theories are being used, we shall omit the subscript.

Since modal logic is constructed as an extension of classical sentence logic, all the results that we developed in that venue, carry over. As hinted above, we can redefine all the interesting proof-conditions and the arguments that they are equivalent are all reusable. So is the notion of a *MAXI* set, though now this idea must be defined relative to a logic L. To signal this we shall use the notation *LMAXI* with $\mathbb{M}_L$ denoting both the class of such and the predicate. In particular we have:

Lemma 3.5.1. [Extension Lemma for Normal Modal Logic] *For all normal modal logics L, for all sets Δ, Δ^+ and for all formulas α:*
$$\Delta \vdash_L \alpha \iff [(\Delta \subseteq \Delta^+ \ \& \ \mathbb{M}_L(\Delta^+)) \implies \Delta^+ \vdash_L \alpha]$$

This connects 'ordinary' provability with provability by *LMAXI*-sets, which is one of the things we shall need again.

But we shall also need to connect models with *LMAXI*-sets. This turns out to be a more complex undertaking.

First, we define the binary relation, sometimes called the *L-canonical* relation, R_L^+ on $\mathbb{T}_L^+$ as follows:

Definition 3.5.2. '$R_L^+ \Delta \Sigma$' for
'$(\forall \alpha)(\Delta \vdash_L \square \alpha \implies \Sigma \vdash_L \alpha P)$'

It should be clear by inspection that this definition of the relation builds in what we want in the way of matching proof conditions with truth conditions, in the sense that it makes one direction of the following lemma trivial:

Lemma 3.5.3. [R_L^+ Lemma]

Let L be a normal modal logic, then:

$$(\forall \Delta \in T_L^+, \forall \alpha)(\Delta \vdash_L \square \alpha \iff$$
$$(\forall \Sigma)(R_L^+ \Delta \Sigma \implies \Sigma \vdash_L \alpha))$$

Proof. The left to right direction of the biconditional holds by virtue of the definition of R_L^+. In the other direction we argue as follows: for Δ and α arbitrary, suppose that $\Delta \nvdash_L \square \alpha$. We show that in this case, the set $\square(\Delta) \cup \{\neg \alpha\}$ must be *L*-consistent, for, if not, then $\square(\Delta) \vdash_L \alpha$ and by [R$\square$], $\square[\square(\Delta)] \vdash_L \square \alpha$. But the set on the left side of $\vdash_L$, is evidently a subset of Δ, and so by [Mon], $\Delta \vdash_L \square \alpha$, contrary to hypothesis.

So let Σ be the fixed theory $(\mathbb{C}_\vdash(\square(\Delta) \cup \{\neg \alpha\}))^+$. Obviously $R_L^+ \Delta \Sigma$, and $\Sigma \nvdash \alpha$, as required. This gives us what we want though our route is a bit more tortuous than it was in the classical case. $\square$

Evidently fixed theories are going to be the syntactical version of points, and hence sets of these will serve as frames, but not *arbitrary* sets. This much is clear: the pair

(T_L^+, R^+) is a frame (usually called the *canonical frame* for the logic L), and a particularly interesting one. If we define a valuation:

Definition 3.5.4. $V_L^+(\alpha, \Delta) = 1 \iff \Delta \vdash_L \alpha$ for α atomic and $\Delta \in T_L^+$

---

and call the resulting model $\mathcal{M}_L$ (the *L-canonical model*), then it is not difficult to show that:

Theorem 3.5.5. [Fundamental Theorem for Normal Modal Logics]

Let L be any normal modal logic, then:

$$\mathcal{M}_L, \Delta \vDash \alpha \iff \Delta \vdash_L \alpha$$

Proof. The proof is by induction on the number of connectives in α. The basis case, in which α is atomic, is handled by the definition of V^+. In the induction step, assume the result for all α having fewer than n connectives, and show for the case in which α has n connectives. If α is a classical compound, this is proved by the corresponding classical arguments. So let α have the form $\square\beta$.

$$\mathcal{M}_K, \Delta \vDash \square\beta$$

$\iff \forall\Sigma : R_L^+\Delta\Sigma \implies \mathcal{M}_K, \Sigma \vDash \beta$, by the truth-condition.

$\iff \forall\Sigma : R_L^+\Delta\Sigma \implies \Sigma \vdash_L \beta$, by the hypothesis of induction.

$\iff \Delta \vdash_L \square\beta$ by Lemma $[R_L^+]$.

$\square$

In a certain sense, which we shall explore, the L-canonical model contains every model (for L). In order to see that, we must show how an arbitrary model (for L) can be *embedded* in $\mathcal{M}_L$. Let $\mathcal{M}$ be a model for L.

Definition 3.5.6. $\Delta_u^{\mathcal{M}} = \{\alpha | \mathcal{M}, u \vDash \alpha\}$

$\Delta_u^{\mathcal{M}}$ is often called the *theory of u in $\mathcal{M}$*.

Proposition 3.5.7. *For every normal modal logic L, if $\mathcal{M}$ is a model for L, then $\Delta_u^{\mathcal{M}}$ is an $LMAXI$-set.*

Proof. $\Delta_u^{\mathcal{M}}$ must be L-consistent since we know that $\Delta_u^{\mathcal{M}} \not\vDash \bot$. Thus we know that $\Delta_u^{\mathcal{M}} \vdash \bot$, only if $\mathcal{M}$ is not a model for L, . So suppose, for *reductio*, that $\alpha \notin \Delta_u^{\mathcal{M}}$ & $\Delta_u^{\mathcal{M}}, \alpha \not\vdash_L \bot$. By the construction of $\Delta_u^{\mathcal{M}}$, $\neg\alpha \in \Delta_u^{\mathcal{M}}$ so L is non-classical, in which case it is not a normal modal logic, contrary to hypothesis. □

This will let us associate points in an arbitrary model for L with points in the L-canonical model. We need to sharpen this to include the frame-relation.

Lemma 3.5.8. [Frame Relation Lemma]

> Let L be a normal modal logic and $\mathcal{M}$ a model for L, then:
>
> $$(\forall u, v \in \mathbb{U})(Ruv \implies R^+\Delta_u^{\mathcal{M}}\Delta_v^{\mathcal{M}})$$

Proof. Assume that Ruv in some arbitrarily chosen model $\mathcal{M}$ for a normal modal logic L. Assume further that for a formula α, $\Delta_u^{\mathcal{M}} \vdash_L \Box\alpha$. We now wish to show that $\Delta_v^{\mathcal{M}} \vdash_L \alpha$. For *reductio* suppose that $\Delta_v^{\mathcal{M}} \not\vdash_L \alpha$ which by $\mathbb{M}_L(\Delta_v^{\mathcal{M}})$ means that $\Delta_v^{\mathcal{M}} \vdash_L \neg\alpha$. Now it cannot be the case that $\mathcal{M}, v \vDash \alpha$, since then $\Delta_u^{\mathcal{M}}$ would fail to be L-consistent. So it must be the case that $\mathcal{M}, u \vDash \neg\Box\alpha$ and by definition, $\Delta_u^{\mathcal{M}} \vdash_L \neg\Box\alpha$. So $\Delta_u^{\mathcal{M}}$ must be L-inconsistent, which is impossible. □

Theorem 3.5.9. [Embedding Theorem 1 for Normal Modal Logic]

> *Let L be a normal modal logic and $\mathcal{M}$ a model for L, then for every formula α and point u:*

$$\Delta_u^{\mathcal{M}} \vdash_L \alpha \iff \mathcal{M}, u \models \alpha$$

Proof. ($\Leftarrow$) (the 'if' direction) This follows at once from the definition of the set $\Delta_u^{\mathcal{M}}$ and the classical rule [R].

($\Rightarrow$) (the 'only if' direction) An easy induction proof, with an appeal to the Frame Relation Lemma in the induction step, establishes the result.

$\square$

This result shows that what we called an 'association' above, is actually an embedding. Hence the name of the theorem.

Theorem 3.5.10. [Canonical Entailment]

> *Suppose L is a normal modal logic. Then:*

$$\Gamma \models^{\mathcal{M}_L} \alpha \iff \Gamma \models_L \alpha$$

Proof. For the '$\Leftarrow$' direction, we must show that for every normal modal logic L, $\mathcal{M}_L$ is a model for L. Suppose to the contrary that for a normal modal logic L, there is some *LMAXI*-set Δ such that $\mathcal{M}_L, \Delta \models \Gamma$ and $\mathcal{M}_L, \Delta \not\models \alpha$ for some Γ, α such that $\Gamma \vdash_L \alpha$. By the fundamental theorem for normal modal logic, Δ must prove every member of Γ (and hence also contain every member of Γ by the theoryhood of Δ) and also prove $\neg\alpha$. But, by hypothesis, $\Gamma \vdash_L \alpha$. It follows, by the monotonicity of '$\vdash_L$,' that $\Delta \vdash_L \alpha$. Hence Δ is not L-consistent, which is impossible if $\mathbb{M}_L(\Delta)$.

For the '$\Rightarrow$' direction, we notice that if $\Gamma \not\models_L \alpha$, there must be some model $\mathcal{M}$ for L such that, for some point u, $\mathcal{M}, u \models \Gamma$ and $\mathcal{M}, u \not\models \alpha$. But then, by the embedding theorem $\Delta_u^{\mathcal{M}} \vdash$

Γ and $\Delta_u^{\mathcal{M}} \nvdash \alpha$. From this and the fundamental theorem for normal modal logics, it follows that $\Gamma \nvDash^{\mathcal{M}_L} \alpha$.

$\square$

At the heart, if not the soul, of the metalogic of (normal) modal logic are the so-called *determination* results, sometimes known as 'completeness' results. According to this idiom, one says of a certain class of models (or of frames) C and a logic L that

---

Definition 3.5.11. *the logic L is determined by the class C if and only if:* $\Gamma \vdash_L \alpha \iff \Gamma \vDash \alpha[C]$

As an example of this, consider the logic K, the smallest normal modal logic. Since every model is a model for K, we can show that

Theorem 3.5.12. *K is determined by the class of all models (or alternatively by the class of all frames).*

by means of the argument:

Proof. $\Gamma \vdash_K \alpha$
$\iff$ $(\forall \Delta)(KMAXI(\Delta)$ and $\Gamma \subseteq \Delta \implies \Delta \vdash_K \alpha)$ by the Extension Lemma.
$\iff$ $\Gamma \vDash^{\mathcal{M}_K} \alpha$ by the Fundamental Theorem
$\iff$ $\Gamma \vDash_K \alpha$ by the Canonical Entailment theorem
$\iff$ $\Gamma \vDash \alpha[C]$ where C is the class of all models, since every model is a model for K.

$\square$

We can see by this little proof that we have actually done much of the work to establish infinitely many such determination results. The only problem is, that we have shown, for every normal modal logic L, that L is determined by the class of models for L.

Suppose that we had some smaller class C of models in mind, smaller that is, than the class of all models, how would we proceed? We would have to establish that something was a model for the logic, if and only if it belonged to the class C. But how to do that? Well, there is a fast way to do it.

What we need in order to show that L is determined by C, is for C to contain models for L (so that the $\Rightarrow$ part of the determination statement holds) sufficient to refute every pair Γ, α such that $\Gamma \nvdash_L \alpha$ (so that the $\Leftarrow$ part holds). But it is easy to see that we can find a single model to do the latter job—or rather *all* the latter jobs at one go. If $\Gamma \nvdash_L \alpha$ then obviously there must be a *LMAXI*-set Δ which contains Γ and $\neg P$. And this is true of every such pair—so all we need show is that $\mathcal{M}_L$ is a member of the class C and the proof is done. There are many examples of this kind of proof. In fact the production of them was a kind of industry during the 1970's.

Four

Modal Logic: General Considerations

4.1 Introduction

In what sense might we say that a modal logic, a sentential one at least, is *classical*? Of course some will aver that modal logic and classical logic are worlds apart, and that 'necessity' is not, and never could be a classical sentence operator. Quine for instance, and some of his students, have famously taken this stance. But a dispassionate observer might hold that in order to be taken seriously, anybody who would close the gate on such and such being a classical connective owes us a convincing account of what makes a connective classical. Quine has himself argued that the classical connectives, or *particles* as he calls them, should be consistent with his well-known 'policy of extensionality.' We might be tempted by such a plea, were it not for the fact that the policy itself now requires a ground. But whether or not, Quine's argument is correct, it doesn't tell against a sentential modal logic, which can be entirely extensional. In fact, if Quine would allow an extensional necessity operator into the classical fold, which we should hasten to emphasize he nowhere does in so many words, then Segerberg[1] is correct calling those modal logics classical which are extensions of the logic the only modal rule of which is:

$$[\text{RE}] \ \vdash \alpha \equiv \beta \ \Longrightarrow \vdash \Box\alpha \equiv \Box\beta$$

where the name of the rule is intended to suggest *rule* [of] *extensionality*.

But rather than enter this interesting debate, we shall raise instead the issue of when it would make sense to say that we have formalized a *classical theory* of some connective. The answer is obvious: a theory of necessity for instance, is classical if it is an extension of classical logic; if, in other words, the notion of provability in the object language obeys the classical rules of proof.

4.2   Classical theories of the truth operator

Before we begin to re-examine necessity, we start with a slightly more general kind of operator, truth. Suppose we encounter a unary operator ϕ. When shall we say that this operator counts as some or other species of *truth*? Once again hard-liners will say that such an operator is interpretable as truth if and only if it satisfies the principle of triviality:

$$[\text{Triv}\phi] \ \vdash \alpha \equiv \phi(\alpha)$$

but we shall be take a softer line than that, though we shall say nothing which a hard-liner would find disagreeable. Here is the set of conditions to which we adhere:

> Idempotency: In other words, $\phi(\phi(\alpha))$ should be the same as $\phi(\alpha)$.

---

[1]see (Segerberg, 1971)

Strong distribution: ϕ should 'distribute strongly' over at least some of the connectives. As an example:

$$\phi(\alpha \wedge \beta) \equiv (\phi(\alpha) \wedge \phi(\beta))$$

And given that the theory of the truth operator is to be classical, the following also seems intuitively motivated.

Duality: $\neg\phi\neg$ should also be a truth operator, which is to say that it should satisfy the same conditions of idempotency and strong distribution as ϕ.

Somebody might wish to add to these conditions in order to make them hew to a harder line. She might insist, for instance that the duality condition be strengthened to require that $\neg\phi\neg$ be *the same* operator as ϕ, and that ϕ distribute strongly over *all* of the classical connectives. Of course those additions make $\phi(\alpha)$ identical to α. Instead, we pursue the idea that there are classical theories of truth-operators distinct from what we might term as the classical theory of 'classically true.'

Obviously, there is a bit of slack here. In particular, it has been left open how many classical connectives have the strong distribution property. So there is a range of 'truth-likeness' here ranging from just one connective, to all the connectives. At one end, the 'just one connective' end, the necessity operator of normal modal logic would count as a truth-operator (depending upon how strict we make duality condition), since it strongly distributes over conjunction. The dual (normal) possibility also strongly distributes over one connective (although it is a different connective, namely disjunction: the dual of conjunction). Though in order to regard all the normal modal operators as truth-operators, we must be prepared to give up strict adherence to the idempotency principle. If we insist on that principle then we are committed to the view that necessary *truth* is formalized only by those logics which extend $KT4$ (usually referred to as $S4$).

At the 'all connectives' end we offer no examples of any operators except for the identity operator[2] i.e. the trivial operator id such that

$$id(\alpha) = \alpha$$

The last condition might take us even farther away from the classical picture, even though we formalize it in a classical way.

> $\phi[\Gamma] \vdash \phi(\alpha)$ must be recognizable as a species of inference.

The motivation for this is clear: if ϕ is a kind of truth, ϕ-truth say, then saying that the ϕ-truth of the premises (classically) guarantees the ϕ-truth of the conclusion, must be saying that there is something like the relation of deduction between the premises and the conclusion. Of course to say this is to recognize that there might be other, non-classical, accounts of deduction. Some of the sting of this recognition is removed by saying that the alternatives are to be formalized in a classical theory. So, in some sense, the classical notions of truth and deduction are *primary*.

What may not be so clear is what is meant by 'a species of inference.' Here again there is room for disagreement. We might say that at least the structural rules must hold, or that [T] and [R] must hold and [M] hold in 'some form' (allowing perhaps for some restriction on full monotonicity). If we are satisfied with this little we shall not have to struggle to establish that the relation, which we call $\vdash^\phi$, is a kind of inference. This is because it is easy to see that

---

[2]which is not to say that there are no such examples. In fact so-called actuality operators or 'jump operators' in multi-dimensional logic, as for example in (Schotch and Payette, 2011) have the strong distribution properties with respect to all the connectives, but such operators will not be discussed in this volume.

$\vdash^{\phi}$ inherits the structural rules from classical provability. More precisely:

Proposition 4.2.1. $\vdash^{\phi}$ *satisfies* [R], [M], *and* [T].

Proof. In each case we can use the classical version of the structural rule. The details:

> Suppose $\alpha \in \Gamma$. Then $\phi\alpha \in \phi[\Gamma]$ and $\phi[\Gamma] \vdash \phi\alpha$ by (classical) [R], i.e. $\Gamma \vdash^{\phi} \alpha$.
>
> Suppose $\Gamma \vdash^{\phi} \alpha$ and $\Gamma \subseteq \Delta$. It follows that $\phi[\Gamma] \subseteq \phi[\Delta]$, and hence by the classical version of [M] $\phi[\Delta] \vdash \phi\alpha$, i.e. $\Delta \vdash^{\phi} \alpha$.
>
> Suppose $\Gamma, \alpha \vdash^{\phi} \beta$ and $\Gamma \vdash^{\phi} \alpha$. Then $\phi[\Gamma], \phi\alpha \vdash \phi\beta$ and $\phi[\Gamma] \vdash \phi\alpha$ (by definition). But then $\phi[\Gamma] \vdash \phi\beta$ by the classical version of [T], i.e. $\Gamma \vdash^{\phi} \beta$.

$\square$

Others might require at least some of the classical connective rules[3] in addition to pet structural rules. One approach would require that in order to qualify as a genuine inference relation, one must be in possession of a cut-elimination theorem and all that such implies.[4]

Suppose that, in a paroxysm of classicality, we require that the species of inference mentioned in the condition be classical provability. Is this merely another way to insist that the only truth operator properly speaking, is the identity operator? It is certainly true that if we require of ϕ:

$$\phi[\Gamma] \vdash \phi(\alpha) \iff \Gamma \vdash \alpha$$

---

[3]Relevance logicians for instance, seem to be particularly keen on conjunction introduction and conditional elimination.

[4]This is one of the requirements of Ian Hacking in a series of papers. See (Hacking, 1979).

then the condition is satisfied by id. But the condition is *also* satisfied by the K □! For the right to left direction, this is just the rule [R□] (with □ for ϕ) and for the left to right direction, a simple semantical argument carries the day. Here it is.

We wish to show that the converse of [R□] is sound, which is to say that:

$$\Box[\Gamma] \vDash \Box\alpha \implies \Gamma \vDash \alpha$$

We shall prove the contrapositive form. Suppose $\Gamma \nvDash \alpha$. Then there must be some model $\mathcal{M}$ and point u, such that $\mathcal{M}, u \vDash \Gamma$ while $\mathcal{M}, u \nvDash \alpha$. We now construct a new model $\mathcal{M}^*$ which has exactly the same underlying set as $\mathcal{M}$ except for containing one point v which does not occur in $\mathcal{M}$. The underlying relation R^* is just R, the underlying relation of $\mathcal{M}$ with one added pair $\langle v, u \rangle$. In other words in the model $\mathcal{M}^*$, the point v has exactly one R^*-successor, namely u. Finally, the valuation V^* exactly matches V, the valuation of $\mathcal{M}$ on every point the two models have in common, and in the case of v, we can let $V^*(\alpha, v)$ be anything at all, for every $\alpha \in \mathbf{At}$. The point v is often said to be 'led in' to the model $\mathcal{M}$ and such arguments as this, are usually called on that account, 'lead in' arguments. It is easy to see, given the absence of any restrictions on R, that it must be the case that $\mathcal{M}^*, v \vDash \Box[\Gamma]$ and $\mathcal{M}^*, v \nvDash \Box\alpha$. In other words, $\Box[\Gamma] \nvDash \Box\alpha$ as required.

This may be as good a ground as one could have for calling K the logic of *logical* necessity.

Having got ourselves a truth operator from somewhere (later, see page 107, we shall give a detailed example of such a getting), we can use it to introduce a notion of necessity. The concept of necessity in question may be characterized as the one which is closed under ϕ-deduction (where ϕ is the truth operator). In other words, we can give the basic proof-theory of this notion of necessity, indicated by $\Box^\phi$, by means of the rule:

$$[\phi\Box^\phi] \; \Gamma \vdash^\phi \alpha \;\Rightarrow\; \Box^\phi[\Gamma] \vdash \Box^\phi\alpha$$

Depending upon the form of the model-theory for the logic, this might generate the truth-condition for $\Box^\phi$. For instance, using set-theoretic semantics of the usual kind—models are sets, with some-or-other structure on them represented by a binary relation, and assignment functions mapping atomic formulas into subsets, we can predict that the following clause:

$$\mathcal{M}, u \vDash \Box^\phi\alpha \;\Longleftrightarrow\; (\forall v)[Ruv \;\Rightarrow\; \mathcal{M}, v \vDash \phi\alpha]$$

will be correct. In this R is the binary relation representing the structure and u, v are elements of the underlying set. By correct here we mean that the rule $[\phi\Box]$ must preserve validity in the class of these models.

Except when he used 'necessarily' as a synonym for 'deductively', as was remarked earlier, Aristotle normally used the notion of necessity, in combination with predication.[5] This mode is now often referred to as the *de re* notion of necessity. There is another notion, the one with which we are mainly concerned, on which necessity is a kind of truth.. The later is sometimes called the *de dicto* notion of necessity. Apart from this one mention, we shall not use the distinction because, in spite of its intuitive appeal, it remains vexed.

Considering the reading 'It is necessarily *true* that α.' for $\Box\alpha$, one is led naturally to the possibility of defining an inference relation by means of:

$$\Gamma \vdash^{\Box\phi} \alpha \;\Longleftrightarrow\; \Box^\phi[\Gamma] \vdash \Box^\phi\alpha$$

---

[5]This should not surprise anybody since Aristotle's logic was centered on *terms* rather than sentences.

This leads directly to the question of the relation between $\vdash^\phi$ and $\vdash^{\Box^\phi}$. We have already noticed one case in which they are equal—the modal logic K, which is determined by the class of all models (alternatively, by the class of all frames). It seems likely that other cases, if they exist, must require logics which are determined by the class of all models of some general sort.

What hangs on this issue—the identity or not of $\vdash^\phi$ and $\vdash^{\Box^\phi}$, is which properties of $\Box^\phi$ are inherited by corresponding properties of ϕ. For example, consider the rules:

$$[\text{RM}\phi] \quad \vdash \alpha \supset \beta \;\Rightarrow\; \vdash \phi\alpha \supset \phi\beta$$
$$[\text{RN}\phi] \quad \vdash \alpha \;\Rightarrow\; \vdash \phi\alpha$$
$$[\text{K}\phi] \quad \vdash \phi\alpha \wedge \phi\beta \supset \phi(\alpha \wedge \beta)$$

It's relatively easy to show:

Proposition 4.2.2. *The ϕ versions of the principles* [RM], [RN], *and* [K] *imply the respective $\Box^\phi$ versions (i.e. the usual versions) where the $\Box^\phi$ is introduced by by the rule* $[\phi\Box^\phi]$.

Proof. Assume that $[\text{RM}\phi]$ holds and assume that $\vdash \alpha \supset \beta$. Then by the rule, $\vdash \phi\alpha \supset \phi\beta$. By the converse of conditional introduction[6] it follows that $\phi\alpha \vdash \phi\beta$. Hence $\alpha \vdash^\phi \beta$ by definition of that relation and so $\Box^\phi\alpha \vdash \Box^\phi\beta$ by $[\phi\Box^\phi]$. Thus $\vdash \Box^\phi\alpha \supset \Box^\phi\beta$ by conditional introduction. The proofs for the other principles are quite similar to this one.   □

We know then that if any of the ϕ principles hold, then so do the corresponding 'ordinary' ones, but we are likely to be interested in what happens when one or more of the ϕ principles *fails*. Does this imply the failure of the corresponding $\Box^\phi$ principle? A bit of thought will show us that such failure will indeed be transmitted to the derived

---

[6]A rule which obviously holds but has never been named.

necessity operator, provided that $\vdash^{\Box\phi}$ implies $\vdash^{\phi}$. The reasoning in each case is obvious.

4.3 Inference without truth

Of course there are other notions of inference than those which can be easily specified via a truth-operator as was done in the last section. In fact for some inference relations, such as intuitionistic inference, the idea of defining provability in terms of truth is distasteful, to say the least. There are also inference relations, some paraconsistent ones for instance, in which truth-preservation is not the whole and only story.[7] For these, and perhaps other notions of inference, we can still introduce an account of necessity in the same way as we have done earlier. In fact, we hold that every genuine inference relation corresponds to some notion of necessity.

---

[7]Although we never seem to run out of *something* to preserve.

Five

Many-Valued Logic

5.1 Introduction

Many-valued logic seems to have developed in the 20th Century, although there were important anticipations in the 19th. In his original work on the algebra of logic, for instance, Boole always considered the general case, and didn't confine himself to the study of the two values 0 and 1. The problem was that he seemed not to have any very compelling interpretation for the intermediate values. His preferred reading of them as probabilities is evidently unhelpful.[1] His contemporaries, W. S. Jevons for example, preferred to simplify truth-value calculations by using only the 2-valued algebra which gave them 'self-evident force and meaning', while the more general calculations, even though they give the same result, do so (according to Jevons) by means of 'dark and symbolic processes.'[2]

The idea that there were only two categories of semantic evaluation, true and false, was attacked by J.S. Mill in his examination of the philosophy of Sir William Hamilton.

---

[1] Since, among other reasons, probabilities cannot be assigned to sentences in a truth-functional way and the intermediate values are so assigned.

[2] Quoted by C.I. Lewis

Hamilton had stated that the so-called law of excluded middle was true even of the noumena. Incensed by this view, Mill rejoins that not only is the principle not a law, it isn't even true, saying:

> 'Between the true and false there is a third possibility, the Unmeaning.'[3]

Mill had in mind here that there are expressions which are grammatically well-formed, and hence count as sentences, but they are neither true nor false. His example is 'Abracadabra is a second intention.' An even better example would be a sentence which commits a *sortal mistake*. For instance:

> The taste of lemon is unbreakable.

Somebody might try to defend the principle of excluded middle by requiring all the 'unmeaning' sentences to be marked false. But if it is false that the taste of lemon in unbreakable, then it must be true that the taste of lemon is breakable, which would cast a noticeable pall over the proposal. It is probably better to do as (in effect) Mill's contemporary critics did, and say that an expression can be grammatical without being a declarative sentence. It seems that in so far as any of the examples really and truly lack meaning, then there cannot be anything which they claim is the case, and so they fail to be the sort of objects which fall within the purview of the logic of sentences.

In the first half of the 20th Century, many-valued logics were developed by Łukasiewicz and his students, especially Tarski, and Wajsberg in Poland. In the united states E.L. Post had introduced a generalization of the two-valued truth-value system in his doctoral thesis.[4]

---

[3](Mill, 1865) p. 416
[4]submitted in 1920 to Columbia University

No area of philosophical logic has suffered so many denunciations from the pulpit as many-valued logic. Nor is it difficult to understand why that should be. Consider one of the (20th Century) central motivations for abandoning the classical view of the truth-values:[5]

There are cases in which we clearly cannot assign either of the values true or false to a certain sentence. Therefore, that sentence must be assigned some value different from truth or falsehood.

This might be called the 'truth-value fallacy,' although the premise is far from fallacious. We can certainly agree, for example, that that there might be sentences the truth-value of which may not be *settled* now.[6] Or at least that one might hold such a view, as part of being a libertarian perhaps, without absurdity. What doesn't follow is the necessity of deploying some other, non-classical, truth-value. If some sentence[7] cannot be assigned truth or falsehood, for whatever reason, it doesn't follow that there is some other value which it can (or must) be assigned.

To put the matter another way, 'neither true nor false' is not the name of a truth-value—not without a lot of argument that is. Anyone who asserts the contrary is going to have to explain why 'both true and false' is not also the name of a truth-value.[8] Or, if one is prepared to bite that particularly nasty bullet, why 'neither true nor false and

---

[5]It isn't as clear as most people seem to think just what the classical position on the truth-values *is*. To assume that classicality means 2 truth-values can't be entirely correct. For one thing it would mean that the classical account of the truth-functions is non-Boolean. This is because a Boolean algebra might have any number of truth-values so long as that number, if finite, is a power of 2. It is very easy to construct a 4-valued semantics which agrees exactly with the 2-valued one, in terms of semantic entailment and logical truth.

[6]Something like this is the original Łukasiewicz motivation for requiring more than the two classical values. See (Łukasiewicz, 1967a)

[7]Assuming, for the moment, that it is not part of the definition of 'declarative sentence' that it be either true or false.

[8]Before we withdraw in revulsion at such an idea, it ought to be mentioned that Nuel Belnap, among others have proposed exactly this scheme.

both true and false' is not the name of a truth-value. It doesn't take the wisdom of Solomon to see where this is heading.

In spite of its dubious intuitive underpinnings however, many-valued logic continues to flourish. In this chapter, we shall consider how best to introduce more truth-values into the semantics of sentence logic. It should be emphasized though, that these new truth-values are to be *added* to the existing ones, rather than replacing them. In fact it is far from clear what it would mean to replace the values 'true' and 'false.' We shall examine the simplest case for the most part, the case in which there is one extra truth value.

5.2   Three-Valued Logic

As must be evident from its name, three-valued logic begins with semantics. It begins, in point of fact, with the truth tables for the connectives.

Semantics

We know how to construct the truth-tables for the connectives with T and F, and this knowledge will be carried along with us when we add another value. The first thing to settle is the name of the 'third.' When the classical values are represented by 1 and 0, the other value is often called '1/2' but we shall use 'I' which suggests 'indeterminate' although we have no very clear idea of how to interpret the value. One thing is certain: mere name calling does not amount to interpretation. This leads one to wonder what *does* amount to interpretation. The issue has haunted generations of many-valued logicians and will form an important part of our study below. To begin with, things look easy. Consider the following table for the conjunction connective, $\wedge$.

β values

$\alpha \wedge \beta$	T	F	I
T	T	F	I
F	F	F	F
I	I	F	I

α values (rows); β values (columns)

In this sort of table, the values which β takes on are listed across the top, the values which α takes on are listed down the left hand side and the values taken on by α ∧ β are found in the table as the intersection of α-values with β-values.

The first thing we notice is that most of the table entries are determined by the fact that T and F are just the classical truth-values. So when either of the conjuncts is false, the entire conjunction must be false, on the classical picture. Similarly, when both the conjuncts are true, then the conjunction is likewise true, looking at matters classically. This just leaves three cases to trouble us: the cases in which one conjunct is true and the other takes the value I and the case in which both conjuncts take the value I. We might allow ourselves to be guided in these cases by the reading of I as 'indeterminate.' Presumably, on a large range of the possible understandings of this term, we simply cannot determine the value of the conjunction in the cases under consideration, which surely suggests that the value I be assigned in all these cases.

Precisely similar musings lead to the following table for the disjunction connective, ∨.

β values

$\alpha \vee \beta$	T	F	I
T	T	T	T
F	T	F	I
I	T	I	I

α values

And the table for negation, ¬, is at least as straightforward as the other two. For how could the negation of an indeterminate be any less indeterminate (or any more)?

α	$\neg\alpha$
T	F
F	T
I	I

But now we come to a watershed—the table for the conditional, $\supset$. In constructing the classical table, one comes to see that the admirable property of truth-functionality is obtained only at a price. In the 3-valued situation the price is nearly unbearable. It all comes down to the question of which value $\alpha \supset \beta$ should be assigned when α and β are both assigned the value I. Were $\supset$ to continue to be regarded as equivalent to $\neg(\alpha \wedge \neg\beta)$, it is easy to compute that since $\neg I = I$, the value of the conditional should be I when both antecedent and consequent take the value I.

Any relief at the ease of this calculation is likely to be short lived however when one realizes that more information than the truth-values of the antecedent and consequent is required, before a truth-value for the conditional can comfortably be assigned. For instance, the I value for the conditional makes sense when the values of the antecedent and consequent are assigned 'independently.' No doubt this notion would be as difficult to specify here as it is in the statistical case, but this much seems clear: when the antecedent *is* the consequent, then it isn't possible to assign different values to the two, and when the value assigned is I, there can be no question that the antecedent and consequent receive the same value *non*-independently.

And in the case in which the antecedent is the same sentence as the consequent, we might be tempted by: It doesn't really matter that the truth-value cannot be determined, whatever it really is, it will be the same for both antecedent and consequent and hence the conditional must receive the value T is this case—which might as well be called the *dependent* case.

Almost no work has been done on a non-truth-functional approach to the evaluation of the 3-valued ⊃. Instead the focus has been on the construction of the 'correct' table.

It should be noticed that in the informal considerations so far, the meaning of 'indeterminate' has been tacitly restricted to that range in which the sentences are regarded as *really* having one of the classical values, but it *cannot be determined*, which. There is also an alternative notion, which might be dubbed the *Copenhagen* or *anti-realist* view. According to this picture, there is no sense to be made in saying that a sentence has a classical truth-value independently of our ability to determine what it is. To say that the classical value cannot be determined is to say that the sentence in question does not take a classical value, that there is no 'fact of the matter' regarding its classical value, hidden from our best efforts to determine it. This undermines the position that when antecedent and consequent are the same sentence, when that sentence takes the value I, the conditional should be assigned the value T.

There is however, another argument which should be canvassed, one which held a great deal of sway in the 20th Century. The argument: Unless the value T is assigned in the table cell representing the case when both antecedent and consequent take I, the formula $\alpha \supset \alpha$ will fail to be logically true (i.e. there will be 3-valued truth-value assignments on which $\alpha \supset \alpha$ does not receive the value T). This is absurd, since the formula in question *is* a logical truth, if anything is. Hence the value in the table for $\alpha \supset \alpha$ when both α and β are assigned I must be T.

Historically, this is the view which was closest to the thinking of the pioneers of many-valued logic, especially

Łukasiewicz[9] and Rosser and Turquette.[10]

This argument says nothing about truth-functionality or assigning T only in the dependent case. It says always assign T no matter what, on pain of losing a central logical truth.

On the other hand, a dedicated anti-realist might very well say that there isn't any way to motivate assigning T to $\alpha \supset \alpha$ when α assumes the value I. There certainly isn't any classical intuition to which we can appeal here, since we cannot say that α is bound to be either T or F and in either case the conditional is T. We can agree with the earlier statement that $\alpha \supset \alpha$ is a logical truth if anything is, but it doesn't follow that $\alpha \supset \alpha$ is, in fact, a logical truth. It is open to us to say under an anti-realist interpretation of the expanded semantics, that there are no logical truths.

We shall call the first conditional defined by the following tables, the Ł3 conditional (since it is the one introduced by Łukasiewicz), While the second conditional will be called the *strong* conditional since it is based on the so-called strong tables introduced by Kleene.[11]

		β values		
	$\alpha \supset \beta$	T	F	I
	T	T	F	I
α values	F	T	T	T
	I	T	I	T

		β values		
	$\alpha \supset \beta$	T	F	I
	T	T	F	I
α values	F	T	T	T
	I	T	I	I

---

[9]This is something of a stretch.   What Łukasiewicz actually says in (Łukasiewicz, 1967b) p. 53 is 'The desired equations I obtained on the basis of detailed considerations which were more or less plausible to me.'

[10]See (Rosser and Turquette, 1952).

[11]see Kleene (1952) pp 334-335

In both cases there will be a corresponding notion of biconditional defined as usual. The Ł3 version is given by this table:

	β values		
$\alpha \equiv \beta$	T	F	I
T	T	F	I
F	F	T	I
I	I	I	T

β values

And the version that corresponds to the strong conditional has this table:

	β values		
$\alpha \equiv \beta$	T	F	I
T	T	F	I
F	F	T	I
I	I	I	I

α values

Using these tables we may define a pair of (semantically presented) logics, which we shall refer to by means of Ł3 and $SK3$. Both logics have in common the language SL of classical sentence logic except that $SK3$ does not have the symbol $\bot$.

The previously introduced notion of an *index* **I** as a subset of the set **At** of atomic sentences, can be recycled here but the notion of the set of truth-value assignments which spans a given index must be changed to accommodate the new value. In the classical semantics we could associate a truth-value assignment with each subset i of an index. We must now use *pairs* of subsets of the index to the same end.

In other words we define truth-value assignments along the lines of

Definition 5.2.1. For each index I and pair $\langle i, j \rangle$ of disjoint subsets of I
$v_{ij}(\alpha) = T$ for every $\alpha \in i$, and $v_{ij}(\beta) = F$ for every $\beta \in j$ and $v_{ij}(\gamma) = I$ for every $\gamma \in I \setminus i \cup j$

We use the analogue of our earlier (classical) notation for the class of all (3-valued) assignments relative to an index I (or *spanning* I) viz. $\mathbb{V}3_I$.

The two logics also share much of the inductive definition of 'truth-value of the formula α relative to a truth-value assignment v_{ij}' which is represented by the notation $\|P\|_{ij}$:

Definition 5.2.2. $\|\alpha\|_{ij}$ is defined inductively for every index I and disjoint subsets i and j of I.

$\|\alpha\|_{ij} = v_{ij}(\alpha)$ if α is atomic.

$\|\alpha \wedge \beta\|_{ij}$, $\|\alpha \vee \beta\|_{ij}$ and $\|\neg\alpha\|_{ij}$ are computed from the (common) tables.

$\|\bot\|_{ij} = F$, for the logic Ł3.

$\|\alpha \supset \beta\|_{ij}$ and $\|\alpha \equiv \beta\|_{ij}$ are computed using the Ł3 conditional and biconditional for the logic Ł3 and

$\|\alpha \supset \beta\|_{ij}$ and $\|\alpha \equiv \beta\|_{ij}$ are computed using the strong conditional and biconditional for the logic $SK3$.

The logics also have in common their understanding of the key logical terms:

Definition 5.2.3. For both logics, $\Gamma \models \alpha$ (Γ entails α) relative to the language indexed by **I** if and only if for every truth-value assignment v_{ij}, if $\|\Gamma\|_{ij} = T$ then $\|\alpha\|_{ij} = T$.

In this definition $\|\Gamma\|_{ij} = T$ abbreviates the statement that every member of Γ assumes the value T relative to the truth-value assignment v_{ij}.

Definition 5.2.4. For both logics, $\models \alpha$ (α is logically true) relative to the language indexed by **I** if and only if $\|\alpha\|_{ij} = T$ for every truth-value assignment in $\mathbb{V}3_\mathbf{I}$.

It is a bit misleading to say that $SK3$ agrees with Ł3 on what constitutes a logical truth. It certainly doesn't follow from that agreement, that the two logics recognize the same logical truths. In point of fact, as was foreshadowed above, $SK3$ doesn't recognize *any* logical truths at all! This is because there are no restrictions on which functions v_{ij} may be truth-value assignments. So for any formula α, there will be an assignment, $v_{\emptyset\emptyset}$ at least and there may well be others, relative to which all the atomic formulas in α assume the value I. But the tables for the compounding operations in $SK3$ assign I whenever all of the component formulas assume I. So relative to this truth-value assignment, α assumes the value I.

Many of the points we wish to make below don't require that we pick some specific index **I** for our language. When we are talking more ambiguously in this way, we generally leave off the subscript from the notation for the truth-value assignment functions.

This situation is of interest as regards a question in the philosophy of logic, in fact one of the most basic such ques-

tions: What is logic about? In chapter 1 we provide two answers. In the tradition of Boole, Russell and Quine, logic is
about the logical truths (theorems or tautologies depending on whether syntax or semantics is paramount). On the
other account, perhaps the most ancient, logic is about the
inferences. The two logics Ł3 and $SK3$ provide an interesting test case. On the former view, the 'laws of thought'
approach as we called it, nothing could be more different
than these two logics, while on the latter the matter isn't
so clear.

Some Consequences of these Definitions

It's easy to see that even if we have logical truths, we won't
have all the classical ones. The fact that only Ł3 conditionals allow the 'destruction' of the value I means that any
non-conditional will always take I under some truth-value
assignment. So $\alpha \vee \neg\alpha$ is no longer a logical truth.

Nor is it only the stock of logical truths which suffers
diminution. Consider the rule of conditional proof (sometimes called the deduction theorem) in semantic guise.

$$\Gamma, \alpha \vDash \beta \implies \Gamma \vDash \alpha \supset \beta$$

Consider the possibility that the antecedent of this rule
might be true because whichever truth-value assignment v
makes Γ all true, makes α assume the value I and at least
one such v makes β assume the value F.

Is such a thing possible? In Ł3 it is.

1. Let Γ be the set $\{\alpha \equiv \neg\alpha, \neg\beta\}$.

2. In Ł3 it is only possible that $\|\alpha \equiv \neg\alpha\|_{ij} = T$ if $\|\alpha\|_{ij} = I$. So

3. Every v_{ij} which makes this particular Γ assume the
   value T, makes α assume I and β assume F. This

means that it is impossible to make Γ together with α all assume the value T. Thus (trivially) it must be the case that Γ together with α entails everything, including β. In classical logic, this would force $\Gamma \vDash \neg\alpha$, which would imply that $\Gamma \vDash \alpha \supset \beta$, but such is not the case in Ł3. Instead:

4. Every v_{ij} that makes Γ assume T makes α assume I and β assume F and thus makes $\alpha \supset \beta$ assume I according to the table for the Ł3 conditional. So

5. $\Gamma \nvDash \alpha \supset \beta$, on the definition of entailment.

This reasoning also exposes the fact that Ł3 does not admit the classical negation rules. From the fact that $\Gamma, \alpha \vDash \bot$ it does not follow in Ł3 that $\Gamma \vDash \neg\alpha$. In the example v_{ij} above, $\|\neg\alpha\|_{ij} = I$ when $\|\Gamma\|_v = T$.

What made this work for Ł3 is the fact that for any formula α, there is a compound $f(\alpha)$, the truth-value of which relative to v_{ij} is such that $f(\alpha)$ assumes the value T exactly when α assumes the value I. It's fairly easy to see that in $SK3$ there is no such function. For consider an arbitrary compound formula $f(\alpha)$. If the compound assumes the value T then it's always possible that α might assume at least one value different from I. So for instance, if f is the identity ($f(\alpha) = \alpha$) then when $f(\alpha) = T$ so does α. The same holds when $f(\alpha)$ is a conjunction (when $f(\alpha)$ is true so is α). When $f(\alpha)$ is a disjunction then when $f(\alpha)$ assumes T, α might assume I but it might equally well assume the value T or the value F. Similarly, when $f(\alpha)$ is a conditional then when $f(\alpha)$ is true, α can be any of the three values. Finally, when $f(\alpha)$ is a biconditional then α can only be either T or F.[12]

---

[12] strictly speaking this 'result' should be proved by an induction on the structure of $f(\alpha)$ but the 'hand-waving' version is enough to convince us for all practical purposes.

But we must be careful not to infer from this that the rule of conditional proof holds for $SK3$. Suppose that for some truth-value assignment v_{ij}, $\|\Gamma\|_{ij} = T$ and $\|\alpha \supset \beta\|_{ij} \neq T$. In classical semantics this would amount to saying the $\alpha \supset \beta$ assumes the value F relative to v_{ij} which in turn would mean that $\|\alpha\|_{ij} = T$ and $\|\beta\|_{ij} \neq T$. And this would show that $\Gamma, \alpha \nvDash \beta$, which would amount to an indirect proof of $\Gamma, \alpha \vDash \beta \implies \Gamma \vDash \alpha \supset \beta$ in $SK3$, if only there weren't also the possibility that $\|\alpha \supset \beta\|_{ij} = I$. But there is that possibility and from $\|\alpha \supset \beta\|_{ij} = I$ it doesn't follow that $\|\alpha\|_{ij} = T$, and hence it no longer follows that $\Gamma, \alpha \nvDash \beta$.

So what is the difference between Ł3 and $SK3$ in this respect? In the former we can prove that conditional proof doesn't preserve entailment, and in the latter we cannot prove that it does.

Proof Theory

Under this heading things go rather differently from the way they go in classical logic. There, proof-theory and semantics are on a more-or-less equal footing. It might even be argued, and certainly has been argued by many proof-theorists, that proof theory is *conceptually prior* to semantics. No such argument is available here. Whatever other benefits proof theory might have, it cannot be prior to semantic insights for 3-valued logic (and many-valued logic in general).

Instead the role of proof theory is to produce the syntax which corresponds to the previously existing semantics. In other words the problem we now take up is to 'solve for $\vdash_X$' in the following equivalence:

$$\Gamma \vdash_X \alpha \iff \Gamma \vDash \alpha$$

How does one do such a thing? Does one attempt to guess the proof-theoretic principles (inference rules or axioms), then try to prove the above equivalence, and make adjustments (or new guesses) when the proof fails until one arrives at last, if at all, at a solution? That approach sounds rather unlikely but it seems that Łukasiewicz and his students pursued a strategy very similar to this (except that the guesses were generally referred to as 'conjectures.'[13]) It is quite startling how many of the conjectures, of Łukasiewicz in particular, were verified in the end.

As beginners however, we don't have the background to form useful conjectures. We can, however, see at once that some principles obviously preserve entailment in both logics. For example:

[R] $\alpha \in \Gamma \implies \Gamma \vdash \alpha$

[M] $\Gamma \vdash \alpha \implies \Gamma \cup \Delta \vdash \alpha$

[T] $[\Gamma, \alpha \vdash \beta \,\&\, \Gamma \vdash \alpha] \implies \Gamma \vdash \beta$

[∧] $[\Gamma \vdash \alpha \,\&\, \Gamma \vdash \beta] \iff \Gamma \vdash \alpha \land \beta$

[∨I] $[\Gamma \vdash \alpha \text{ or } \Gamma \vdash \beta] \implies \Gamma \vdash \alpha \lor \beta$

[∨E] $[\Gamma \vdash \alpha \lor \beta \,\&\, \Gamma, \alpha \vdash \gamma \,\&\, \Gamma, \beta \vdash \gamma] \implies \Gamma \vdash \gamma$

[⊃E] $[\Gamma \vdash \alpha \supset \beta \,\&\, \Gamma \vdash \alpha] \implies \Gamma \vdash \beta$

[≡E] $[\Gamma \vdash \alpha \equiv \beta \,\&\, \Gamma \vdash \alpha] \implies$
$\Gamma \vdash \beta$ and $[\Gamma \vdash \alpha \equiv \beta \,\&\, \Gamma \vdash \beta] \implies \Gamma \vdash \alpha$

Both double negation and the so-called De Morgan replacement rules are also correct for both logics. In other words:

[DN] $\alpha \longleftrightarrow \neg\neg\alpha$

[DM] $\neg(\alpha \lor \beta) \longleftrightarrow \neg\alpha \land \neg\beta$

---

[13] A conjecture would seem to be something like an *informed* guess.

[DM] $\neg(\alpha \wedge \beta) \longleftrightarrow \neg\alpha \vee \neg\alpha$

This is evidently not enough proof-theory for equivalence. How could one enlarge the set of rules until it suffices? One thing we can do, although it is not particularly elegant[14] is to 'read off' from the truth-tables for the connectives a set of replacement rules. Apart from that, it is often said that the way to arrive at an equivalence of the above sort is 'replicate the semantics inside the syntax.' We shall try to do something similar here.

In particular, we shall formulate a syntactical version of 'α assumes a classical value, relative to v' and 'α assumes the value I relative to v. It turns out that such a strategy works well for Ł3. For $SK3$, we shall need to try something a bit different.

Proof Theory and Metalogic for Ł3

What counts as the correct proof theory for Ł3 will depend centrally upon whether or not the proposed account of 'proves' matches the previously given account of 'entails' for Ł3. It is for this reason that one does the proof theory in tandem with the metalogic.

We have an idea, from our consideration of the fate of the rule of conditional proof, of how to say in the object language that a formula α assumes the value I, viz. $\alpha \equiv \neg\alpha$. This formula assumes the value T relative to a truth-value assignment v if and only if α assumes the value I, relative to v. This will be such a useful notion that we introduce an abbreviation.

Notation . For any formula α, $I(\alpha)$ abbreviates $\alpha \equiv \neg\alpha$.

It should be clear that Ł3 enjoys the usual negation rules:

---

[14]Georg Cantor, a pioneer of set theory, is said to have remarked 'Elegance is the concern of shoemakers and tailors.' by which we are meant to understand that it is not a concern of mathematicians or philosophers.

[⊥I] [$\Gamma \vdash \alpha \,\& \, \Gamma \vdash \neg\alpha$] $\Rightarrow$ $\Gamma \vdash \perp$

[⊥E] $\Gamma \vdash \perp$ $\Rightarrow$ $\Gamma \vdash \alpha$

It also has two which are peculiar to Ł3

[⊥Ł3I1] [$\Gamma \vdash \alpha \,\& \, \Gamma \vdash I(\alpha)$] $\Rightarrow$ $\Gamma \vdash \perp$

[⊥Ł3I2] [$\Gamma \vdash \neg\alpha \,\& \, \Gamma \vdash I(\alpha)$] $\Rightarrow$ $\Gamma \vdash \perp$

We also have an idea of how to express a sort of classical negation 'α is not true', (which is equivalent to 'α is false' in classical sentence logic, but not in Ł3) viz. $\alpha \supset \neg\alpha$. This was referred to as 'classical' just now because it can assume only the values T and F. In fact, we shall introduce an abbreviation for the latter expression:

Notation . $\overline{\alpha}$ abbreviates $\alpha \supset \neg\alpha$.

Notice that

$\overline{\overline{\alpha}}$ is not identical to α. And

the replacement rules

$$\overline{\alpha} \wedge \overline{\beta} \longleftrightarrow \overline{\alpha \vee \beta}$$
$$\overline{\alpha} \vee \overline{\beta} \longleftrightarrow \overline{\alpha \wedge \beta}$$

are correct for Ł3. Also, it is evident that

[$\Gamma \vdash \alpha \,\& \, \Gamma \vdash \overline{\alpha}$] $\Rightarrow$ $\Gamma \vdash \perp$ and that the classical negation rules hold for 'bar', i.e.

[‾I] $\Gamma, \alpha \vdash \perp$ $\Rightarrow$ $\Gamma \vdash \overline{\alpha}$

[‾E] $\Gamma, \overline{\alpha} \vdash \perp$ $\Rightarrow$ $\Gamma \vdash \alpha$

In addition we can produce a new set of Ł3 replacement rules using the new abbreviation, by translating the truth-tables using α for α is true, $\neg\alpha$ for α is false, and $I(\alpha)$ for α takes the value I. Here is the result of such a translation:

[I∧] $(\alpha \wedge I(Q)) \vee (\beta \wedge I(\alpha)) \vee (I(\alpha) \wedge I(\beta)) \longleftrightarrow I(\alpha \wedge \beta)$

[I∨] $(\neg\alpha \wedge I(\beta)) \vee (\neg\beta \wedge I(\alpha)) \vee (I(\alpha) \wedge I(\beta)) \longleftrightarrow I(\alpha \vee \beta)$

[Ł3⊃1] $\alpha \supset \beta \longleftrightarrow (\neg\alpha \vee \beta) \vee (I(\alpha) \wedge I(\beta))$

[¬⊃] $\neg(\alpha \supset \beta) \longleftrightarrow (\alpha \wedge \neg\beta)$

[I⊃] $(\alpha \wedge I(\beta)) \vee (I(\alpha) \wedge \neg\beta) \longleftrightarrow I(\alpha \supset \beta)$

[Ł3I] $I(\alpha \longleftrightarrow I(\neg\alpha)$

Finally we have one replacement rule involving $\perp$ viz.

[¬⊥] $\neg P \longleftrightarrow P \supset \perp$

This gives us a way to proceed then, at least in rough
outline: Try to construct the proof-theoretic equivalent of
a truth-value assignment in the same way that one does
this in classical logic. The hard part of this, is that we don't
actually have any proof-theory beyond the bare handful of
rules mentioned in the previous section. The thing to do
then is to see, as we go, which proof-theoretic principles
we shall need, and then show that each of these preserve
entailment in Ł3.

We begin with theories (again). An Ł3 theory is just like
an ordinary theory, except the ordinary notion of provability is replaced by the Ł3 variety, which is indicated by the
notation $\vdash_{Ł3}$. In other words:

Definition 5.2.5. The set Δ is an Ł3 theory, written
TH3(Δ), if and only if, for every formula α:
$\Delta \vdash_{Ł3} \alpha \implies \alpha \in \Delta$.

One way to construct a theory from a given set of formulas is to add all the consequences. Just as in classical logic,
the operation which does this is called deductive closure.

Definition 5.2.6. For every set Δ of formulas, $\mathbb{C}_{\vdash_{L3}}(\Delta) = \{\alpha | \Delta \vdash_{L3} \alpha\}$.

On the way to replicating the semantics inside the syntax, we once again appeal to the notion of a diagram, making the obvious changes to deal with the extra value.

Definition 5.2.7. Given an index $\mathbf{I}$ and a pair of disjoint subsets $\langle i, j \rangle$ of $\mathbf{I}$, we define
$\mathbb{D}_{ij} = \{\alpha \in \mathbf{I} | \alpha \in i\} \cup \{\neg \beta | \beta \in \mathbf{I} \,\&\, \beta \in j\} \cup \{I(\gamma) | \gamma \in \mathbf{I} | \gamma \notin i \,\&\, \gamma \notin j\}$

Given an index $\mathbf{I}$, the class of all diagrams as above, the class of diagrams which *span* $\mathbf{I}$, is denoted by $\mathbb{D}_{\mathbf{I}}$.

Evidently these 3-valued diagrams correspond, in an obvious way, with 3-valued truth-value assignments. This will be the subject of a proof of course, but first we enquire into the properties of the theories we obtain by taking the (3-valued) deductive closure of diagrams.

Any results on these theories will be idle unless they can be shown to be consistent. This follows, as it does classically, from the principle that there can be no logical relations between distinct atomic sentences and the structural rule [T] of transitivity or 'cut.'[15] The construction of the correct version of the former rule (called [W] in chapter 1) for the logic Ł3 is left to the reader.

The first thing we notice is that the closure of any diagram decides every formula, though the meaning of this term has changed slightly from its classical meaning.

---

[15]Since this rule assures that the consequences of the deductive closure of a set must also be consequences of the set. So if the consequences of a diagram are inconsistent so must be the diagram. However in order for a diagram to be inconsistent, there would have to be logical relations between distinct atomic sentences, which is forbidden by [W].

Definition 5.2.8. An Ł3-theory T is said to *Ł3-decide* a formula α if and only if
$T \vdash_{Ł3} \alpha$ or $T \vdash_{Ł3} \neg\alpha$ or $T \vdash_{Ł3} I(\alpha)$

Less formally, a theory decides a formula if it does to the formula what a diagram does to an atomic formula. This is true whether we are talking about classical logic or 3-valued logic. We won't be surprised then if taking the Ł3-theory of a diagram Ł3-decides every formula. On the way to this, we first introduce the notation $\mathbb{T}_{ij}$ for the Ł3-theory of $\mathbb{D}_{ij}$ and $\mathbb{T}_I$ for the class of Ł3-theories of all the members of $\mathbb{D}_I$.

Theorem 5.2.9 (Ł3-Completeness Theorem). *Where* I *is an index, for every* $\mathbb{T}_{ij} \in \mathbb{T}_I$, $\mathbb{T}_{ij}$ *Ł3-decides every formula* α *of the langauge based on that index.*

Proof. Suppose that for some formula α, $\mathbb{T}_{ij}$ fails to decide α for some pair $\langle i, j \rangle$. We shall show by cases that $\mathbb{T}_{ij}$ fails to decide some subformula of α.

[∧] Suppose α is of the form $\beta \wedge \gamma$. It is easy to see by the rules that if $\mathbb{T}_{ij}$ decides both β and γ, then it must decide their conjunction. When the decision involves I this is clear from the new replacement rules and otherwise we reason classically. For example, if $\mathbb{T}_{ij} \vdash \neg\beta$ then $\mathbb{T}_{ij} \vdash \neg\beta \vee \neg\gamma$ and so $\mathbb{T}_{ij} \vdash \neg(\beta \wedge \gamma)$.

The other cases are similar.

But if failure to decide some formula implies failure to decide at least one sub-formula, then we are led inevitably to the failure to decide at least one atomic formula, since formulas are of finite length. But by definition of $\mathbb{D}_{ij}$ it is impossible that $\mathbb{T}_{ij}$ fail to decide any atomic formula. $\square$

Another very useful property of these theories is the previously introduced notion of *primeness*.

Theorem 5.2.10 (Ł3 Primeness Theorem). *For every*
$\mathbb{T}_{ij} \in \mathbb{T}_I : \mathbb{T}_{ij} \vdash \alpha \vee \beta \iff \mathbb{T}_{ij} \vdash \alpha$ *or* $\mathbb{T}_{ij} \vdash \beta$

Proof. The right to left direction holds, as it does classically, by virtue of the rule of disjunction introduction. For the other direction we argue indirectly again. Suppose $\mathbb{T}_{ij} \vdash \alpha \vee \beta$, but neither $\mathbb{T}_{ij} \vdash \alpha$ nor $\mathbb{T}_{ij} \vdash \beta$.

By the completeness property, we know that $\mathbb{T}_{ij}$ must prove one of $\neg\alpha$ or $I(\alpha)$ and the same holds for β. But we can see that $\mathbb{T}_{ij}$ couldn't prove the negations of α and β since it would then prove the negation of $\alpha \vee \beta$, contra the consistency of $\mathbb{T}_{ij}$. Similar considerations apply to $I(\alpha)$ and $I(\beta)$. The proof of those would assure the proof of $I(\alpha \vee \beta)$ and once again $\mathbb{T}_{ij}$ would be inconsistent. Precisely the same consideration applies to the cases in which the theory proves the negation of one disjunct, and the I of the other, thanks to the new replacement rules. It follows then, that $\mathbb{T}_{ij}$ must prove α or β after all. $\square$

We next define a maximally Ł3-consistent set of formulas by analogy with the classical case as follows:

Definition 5.2.11. Σ is an maximally Ł3-consistent set of formulas of the language SL_I, written $\mathbb{M}_{Ł3}(\Sigma)$ or $\Sigma \in \mathbb{M}_{Ł3}$ if and only if:

$\Sigma \nvdash_{Ł3} \bot$ and

$\alpha \notin \Sigma \implies \Sigma, \alpha \vdash_{Ł3} \bot$

By (harmless) abuse of notation, $\mathbb{M}_{Ł3}$ refers indifferently to the class of all maximally Ł3-consistent sets of formulas, as well as to the predicate of being a member of that class.

From this point on the subscript Ł3 will be dropped whenever it is clear from the context which notion of provability is active.

We should notice that, by using essentially the classical reasoning:

Proposition 5.2.12. *Every maximal Ł3-consistent set is a theory*

Next we relate $\mathbb{M}_{Ł3}$ and $\mathbb{T}_{\mathbf{I}}$ assuming, of course that the maximal sets are constructed from the formulas of $SL_{\mathbf{I}}$ (from now on when it is clear from the context, we shall omit explicit mention of this qualification). The first thing we wish to show is that all the members of $\mathbb{T}_{\mathbf{I}}$ are maximal.

Theorem 5.2.13. *For every index* $\mathbf{I}$ *and every* $\mathbb{T}_{ij} \in \mathbb{T}_{\mathbf{I}}$: $\mathbb{M}_{Ł3}(\mathbb{T}_{ij})$

Proof. Assume that $\alpha \notin \mathbb{T}_{ij}$. Since $\mathbb{T}_{ij}$ decides every formula (in the Ł3 sense of that term) it follows that either

$$\mathbb{T}_{ij} \vdash \neg\alpha \text{ or } \mathbb{T}_{ij} \vdash I(\alpha)$$

In either case however, the addition of α to $\mathbb{T}_{ij}$ would result in inconsistency. $\square$

We can also show that the maximal sets in this sense have the Ł3-completeness property.

The proof will require that we have on hand the Ł3 version of conditional proof. The problem with the classical version as noted on page 78, comes when α takes the value I. In that case $\alpha \supset \beta$ might also take the value I. This can be fixed in Ł3 (but not in $SK3$) since we have a way there of ridding ourselves of inconvenient I values—form a conditional with something else that takes I. The Ł3 table for $\supset$ has T where both the antecedent and consequent are I. This suggests a solution to the CP problem, since we already know of a formula which takes I when $\alpha \supset \beta$ does, namely α. Furthermore, relative to any truth-value assignment v, α, never takes T when $\alpha \supset \beta$ takes I or F and never takes I when $\alpha \supset \beta$ takes F. All of which is to say that the following rule preserves entailment in Ł3.

$$[\supset Ł3]\ \Gamma, \alpha \vdash \beta \implies \Gamma \vdash \alpha \supset (\alpha \supset \beta)$$

This rule is sometimes called the 'stuttering' version of CP.

Theorem 5.2.14. [*Completeness of Maximal Ł3-consistent sets*] *Suppose for some formula α of SL_I, $\mathbb{M}_{Ł3}(\Delta)$ & $\Delta \nvdash \alpha$ & $\Delta \nvdash \neg\alpha$ then $\Delta \vdash I(\alpha)$*

Proof. Since $\mathbb{M}_{Ł3}(\Delta)$, it follows that $\Delta, \alpha \vdash \bot$ and similarly that $\Delta, \neg\alpha \vdash \bot$. But then $\Delta \vdash \alpha \supset (\alpha \supset \bot)$ and $\Delta \vdash \neg\alpha \supset (\neg\alpha \supset \bot)$ by the Ł3 version of CP. Applying rules of replacement, we get: $\Delta \vdash \alpha \supset \neg\alpha$ and $\Delta \vdash \neg\alpha \supset \alpha$. But these two together amount to $\Delta \vdash I(\alpha)$. $\square$

We also have the converse, another classical echo.

Proposition 5.2.15. *For every (Ł3-consistent) Ł3-theory Δ, if Δ is Ł3-complete, then $\mathbb{M}_{Ł3}(\Delta)$.*

Proof. Suppose that $\alpha \notin \Delta$. It must be shown that $\Delta, \alpha \vdash \bot$ (by hypothesis, Δ is consistent). Since (by hypothesis) Δ is Ł3-complete, $\Delta \vdash \alpha$ or $\Delta \vdash \neg\alpha$ or $\Delta \vdash I(\alpha)$. The first is impossible since if $\Delta \vdash \alpha$ then $\alpha \in \Delta$ by theoryhood. In either of the other cases, $\Delta, \alpha \vdash \alpha$ and $\Delta, \alpha \vdash \neg\alpha$ so $\Delta, \alpha \vdash \bot$. So $\mathbb{M}_{Ł3}(\Delta)$ as required. $\square$

Evidently the Ł3 flavor of maximal consistency won't entirely coincide with the classical. For example, such sets won't normally be *complete* in the classical sense detailed on page 15, i.e. it will *not* be the case that:

For every formula α and every $\mathbb{M}_{Ł3}$ set Δ, either $\Delta \vdash \alpha$ or $\Delta \vdash \neg\alpha$.

To see this, we first give the usual (classical) construction for producing a maximal Ł3-consistent set starting from an arbitrary Ł3-consistent one, Σ. Let all the formulas of SL_I be confined to an 'urn.' We shall draw the formulas one by one, δ_1 being the first, δ_2 the second, and so on. Once a formula has been drawn, it is not replaced. We shall continue to draw from the urn until it is empty. Relative to this procedure, we define a sequence of sets inductively as follows:

$$\Sigma_0 = \Sigma$$

$\vdots$

$$\Sigma_k = \begin{cases} \Sigma_{k-1} \cup \{\delta_k\} & \text{if this is Ł3-consistent,} \\ \Sigma_{k-1} & \text{otherwise.} \end{cases}$$

$\vdots$

Definition 5.2.16. Σ^+ denotes the set $\bigcup_i \Sigma_i$.

In general where Δ is a(n Ł3-consistent) set, Δ^+ represents the (not usually unique) expansion of Δ using the procedure just given. That the expansion is not unique follows from the fact that that formulas are drawn randomly from the urn and, depending upon the specific composition of the starting set, each iteration of the procedure might result in a distinct expansion.[16]

It is easy to verify, using the classical reasoning pretty much intact, that $\mathbb{M}_{Ł3}(\Sigma^+)$.

Consider the set $\Delta = \{I(\alpha)\}$ (in other words $\{\alpha \equiv \neg\alpha\}$). If we expand this to maximality using the construction,

---

[16]Of course when the starting set is already in $\mathbb{M}_{Ł3}$ then that starting set will be the unique result of the construction no matter in which order the formulas are drawn.

then Δ^+ cannot prove either α or $\neg\alpha$ without proving the other, and hence proving $\bot$.

Having obtained the result that each member of $\mathbb{T}_I$ is (Ł3) maximal, we would now like to show that the converse result holds. In other words:

Theorem 5.2.17. [*Equivalence of* $\mathbb{M}_{Ł3}$ *and* T_I] *For every set* Δ, *of formulas of* SL_I,
$\mathbb{M}_{Ł3}(\Delta) \implies$ *there is some disjoint pair of subsets of* $\mathbf{I}$, $\langle i, j \rangle$ *such that* $T_{ij} = \Delta$.

Proof. The obvious pair here is

$$\langle \{\alpha \in \mathbf{I} | \Delta \vdash \alpha\}, \{\beta \in \mathbf{I} | \Delta \vdash \neg\beta\} \rangle$$

It is easy to see that when $\langle i, j \rangle$ is the latter pair of sets, then by reasoning involving the structural rule [T], if $\mathbb{T}_{ij} \vdash \alpha$ then so must $\mathbb{D}_{ij}$.

In order for the proof to work, we must now be assured that

$$\mathbb{D}_{ij} \subseteq \Delta$$

since then $\Delta \vdash \alpha$ by monotonicity.
By definition

$$\mathbb{D}_{ij} = \{\alpha \in i\} \cup \{\neg\beta | \beta \in j\} \cup \{I(y) | y \in \mathbf{I} \,\&\, y \notin i \,\&\, y \notin j\}$$

We can see that the first two components of this set are included in Δ by definition, so all that remains is to show that that the third component is also included. What we have is that $\Delta \nvdash y$ (else y would be in i) and that $\Delta \nvdash \neg y$ (else y would be in j). Since Δ is $\mathbb{M}_{Ł3}$ it has the Ł3-completeness property by theorem 5.2.14, hence:

$$\Delta \vdash I(y)$$

so $I(y) \in \Delta$ and hence $\mathbb{D}_{ij} \subseteq \Delta$ as required.

This shows that $\mathbb{T}_{ij} \subseteq \Delta$. But since $\mathbb{M}_{\text{Ł}3}(\mathbb{T}_{ij})$ and $\mathbb{M}_{\text{Ł}3}(\Delta)$ it must follow that $\mathbb{T}_{ij} = \Delta$. $\square$

At this point we have accumulated enough proof theory to begin reconstructing the semantics. This too is relatively close to the classical procedure. Given an index **I**, we previously defined the notion of a truth-functional extension of a subset i of **I** and then showed that such extensions were unique. What we shall do now is to enlarge the previous definition to the notion of a *truth-tabular extension* of a pair $\langle i, j \rangle$ of subsets of some index **I**. This change is entirely cosmetic since the classical assignment of truth-values can also be realized by means of truth-tables. Once we extend an initial distribution of (however many) truth-values to an index **I** to all formulas of $SL_{\mathbf{I}}$ by means of a table (for each connective) such extensions are clearly unique. This is because the value of a compound formula depends exactly on the values of its components. Thus if two compound formulas take different values relative to two truth-tabular extensions, the two cannot both extend the same pair $\langle i, j \rangle$. In other words:

Proposition 5.2.18 (Uniqueness of Truth-Tabular Extensions). *Let X and Y be two truth-tabular extensions of the pair $\langle i, j \rangle$ of disjoint subsets of the index **I** by means of the same table for each connective, then X and Y assign the same value to every formula of $SL_{\mathbf{I}}$.*

One can now prove that what holds by definition for the atomic formulas, holds by properties of provability or of maximality, for all formulas.

Theorem 5.2.19 (Correspondence Theorem for Ł3). *For every index **I**, every pair of disjoint subsets of **I**, $\langle i, j \rangle$ and every formula α,*

$$\|\alpha\|_{ij} = \begin{cases} T & \Longleftrightarrow & \mathbb{T}_{ij} \vdash \alpha \\ F & \Longleftrightarrow & \mathbb{T}_{ij} \vdash \neg\alpha \\ I & \Longleftrightarrow & \mathbb{T}_{ij} \vdash I(\alpha) \end{cases}$$

Proof. This result follows from the uniqueness of truth-tabular extensions along with the (admittedly tedious) proof that $\mathbb{T}_{ij}$ *is* a truth tabular extension of the pair $\langle i, j \rangle$ which uses the same tables as $\|P\|_{ij}$. The latter proof is left as an exercise, but the reader should notice that the new replacement rules for instance, will have an important role to play. $\qquad\Box$

Theorem 5.2.20 (Equivalence Theorem for Ł3). *The following are equivalent for every language S_I.*

(1) $\Gamma \vdash \alpha$

(2) $\Gamma \vDash \alpha$

(3) for every $\langle i, j \rangle \in \mathbf{I} : \|\Gamma\|_{ij} = T \implies \|\alpha\|_{ij} = T$

(4) for every $\mathbb{T}_{ij} \in \mathbb{T}_{\mathbf{I}} : \Gamma \subseteq \mathbb{T}_{ij} \implies \mathbb{T}_{ij} \vdash \alpha$

Proof. Much of the classical proof can be reused here. For example:

(2) $\Longleftrightarrow$ (3) holds since (3) is just the definition of (2).

(4) $\Longleftrightarrow$ (1) by using the classical argument with—for $\neg$. In other words: $\Leftarrow$ holds in virtue of the rule [M] of monotonicity. For $\Rightarrow$, suppose $\Gamma \nvdash \alpha$. Then $\Gamma \cup \{\overline{\alpha}\}$ must be consistent, otherwise $\Gamma \vdash \alpha$. Expand the latter set to a member of $\mathbb{M}_{Ł3}$, say Γ^+ which we know to be a member of $T_{\mathbf{I}}$ by theorem 5.2.17 and clearly $\Gamma^+ \nvdash \alpha$.

(3) $\Longleftrightarrow$ (4) requires the earlier correspondence result.

$\qquad\Box$

Proof Theory and Metalogic for $SK3$

We shall continue to use expressions like SL_I to refer to a language generated from the index $\mathbf{I} \subseteq \mathbf{At}$, but when we are concerned with $SK3$, the reader should take care to note that the symbol $\perp$ does not appear.

In spite of the fact that the replacement rule:

$$[SK3\text{imp}]\ \alpha \supset \beta \longleftrightarrow \neg\alpha \vee \beta$$

holds for $SK3$ and not for Ł3, it is not the case that the former logic is 'more classical' than the latter. If anything, the opposite is true.

Apart from the fact that there are no logical truths in $SK3$ unless we change the definition of logical truth (which should be approached only with a great deal of fear and trembling), we cannot characterize the truth-values in the object language.

In Ł3 there is a formula which takes the value T only when α takes the value T, a formula which takes the value T only when α takes the value F and also a formula which takes the value T only when α takes the value I. These are respectively: α, $\neg\alpha$, and $I(\alpha)$. The first two work in $SK3$ for T and F, but nothing works for I, as was remarked on page 79. The best that we can do in $SK3$ is to represent 'α takes a classical value' by means of the formula:

$$\alpha \vee \neg\alpha$$

and write $\mathbb{C}(\alpha)$ to abbreviate the latter. It should be clear that 'takes a classical value' has the properties we expect. In particular:

$$[\mathbb{C}\neg]\ \Gamma \vdash \mathbb{C}(\alpha) \iff \Gamma \vdash \mathbb{C}(\neg\alpha)$$

$$[\mathbb{C}\vee 1]\ [\Gamma \vdash \mathbb{C}(\alpha)\ \&\ \Gamma \vdash \mathbb{C}(\beta)] \implies \Gamma \vdash \mathbb{C}(\alpha \vee \beta)$$

$[\mathbb{C} \vee 2]\ \Gamma \vdash \neg(\alpha \vee \beta) \implies \Gamma \vdash \mathbb{C}(\alpha) \wedge \mathbb{C}(\beta)$

Using this notion we may give a conditional introduction rule for $SK3$, but not a 'pure'[17] one. The rule in question is:

$[SK3 \supset I]\ \Gamma, \alpha \vdash \beta \implies \Gamma, \mathbb{C}(\alpha) \vdash \alpha \supset \beta$

Having only this partial conditional introduction mechanism together with having no two-valued negation analogous to the 'bar' negation of Ł3, means that almost none of the previous work can be re-used. In particular we can no longer associate the formula $\alpha \equiv \neg\alpha$ with 'the formula α takes the value I.' As we have remarked, there is no formula which can do that job in $SK3$, in the sense of taking the value T relative to any v_{ij} if and only if α takes I relative to that v_{ij}. Instead, for the new version of maximal consistent sets, we shall have to identify the third value I with 'neither $\Sigma \vdash \alpha$ nor $\Sigma \vdash \neg\alpha$.' This is actually equivalent to the Ł3 method, but only *in* Ł3. In other words:

For every $\Sigma \in \mathbb{M}_{Ł3}$ and formula α

$\Sigma \nvdash \alpha \implies \Sigma, \alpha \vdash \perp \implies \Sigma \vdash \alpha \supset \neg\alpha$

$\Sigma \nvdash \neg\alpha \implies \Sigma, \neg\alpha \vdash \perp \implies \Sigma \vdash \neg\alpha \supset \alpha$

So if neither of the above, then $\Sigma \vdash \alpha \equiv \neg\alpha$

But this argument is not available in $SK3$. We *can* re-use the earlier arguments which establish that maximally consistent sets are prime theories, but this doesn't help much if we can't establish that if $\Gamma \nvdash \alpha$ then $\Gamma \cup \{not(\alpha)\}$ is $SK3$ consistent, where $not(\alpha)$ is some formula which

---

[17]This is the sense of pure in which the rule mentions only the operator being introduced. Before shuddering with revulsion, we should notice that (1) there are no reasons beyond the aesthetic ones, for insisting on such rules and (2) The rule for introducing $\perp$ is similarly impure.

takes T relative to any truth-value assignment v_{ij} if and only if α takes a value different from T. The reason of course is that, in $SK3$ no formula takes T when α takes I. We must take a step back and ask just what it is we need to establish.

For any set of formulas Σ and formula α, such that $\Sigma \nvdash \alpha$ there must be a prime theory which contains Σ and which also does not prove α. From what was said just above, it seems that it is going to have to be the *construction*[18] which assures all of

1. theoryhood

2. primeness, and

3. non-provability of α.

Given a set Σ, of formulas of SL_I, a formula y of the same language—the *omitted formula*—such that $\Sigma \nvdash y$, we construct a set using the following recipe. First we have an (idealized) 'urn' which contains all the formulas of SL_I. We then begin to draw formulas (at random) from the urn and add such as are consequences of the set we have built up so far. In this construction, as opposed to the previous classical version, each time we empty the urn, we fill it up once more and continue trying to add formulas to the set we are building up. We stop after the iteration in which we add no new formulas at all. The reason for this change in procedure is to make sure we add at least one disjunct when we add a disjunction, and in later additions we shall be sure to add the consequences of the disjunct. We can make this more precise by saying:

---

[18]I first encountered this idea in the work of Lapierre and Lepage. See Lapierre and Lepage (1999).

Definition 5.2.21. Define the set Σ^+ to be the union of the following sequence where δ_k is the kth formula to be drawn from the urn.

$$\Sigma_0 = \Sigma$$

$\vdots$

$$\Sigma_k = \begin{cases} \Sigma_{k-1} & \text{if} \quad \Sigma_{k-1} \nvdash \delta_k \\ \Sigma_{k-1} \cup \{\delta_k\} & \text{if} \quad \Sigma_{k-1} \vdash \delta_k \\ & \text{unless} \quad \delta_k = \alpha \vee \beta \quad \text{in which case} \\ \Sigma_{k-1} \cup \{\delta_k\} \cup \{\alpha\} & \text{if} \quad \Sigma_{k-1}, \alpha \nvdash \gamma \quad \text{and} \\ \Sigma_{k-1} \cup \{\delta_k\} \cup \{\beta\} & \text{otherwise} \end{cases}$$

$\vdots$

In this construction we never add a formula that isn't proved unless as a disjunct, but we only add a disjunct if the result doesn't prove γ. We should assure ourselves that this part of the construction actually works. We notice that if a disjunction gets added we only test that the first disjunct doesn't prove γ and if it does, we add the second disjunct without testing, since we must add at least one disjunct for every disjunction or lose the primeness property. If the second disjunct also proves γ, then the construction will result in $\Sigma_k \vdash \gamma$.

But then $\Sigma_{k-1} \vdash \gamma$ by [$\vee$E]. So the only way a certain stage of the construction proves γ requires an earlier stage to prove γ. This works back to a stage (the 0th stage for instance) for which it already known that the set at that stage does not prove γ, which is impossible.

So it should be clear that $\Sigma^+ \nvdash \gamma$ since it wasn't a consequence of the base set and only consequences get added or formulas that won't allow γ to become a consequence. Notice that this implies that Σ^+ is $SK3$-consistent (since otherwise it would prove everything). It should also be clear from the construction that Σ^+ is a theory.

Clearly the construction also ensures that Σ^+ is prime.

There is a kind of maximality here, that might be characterized as *relative to* the formula y.

Notation . $\Sigma^+ = \mathbb{M}(\Sigma, y)$ for 'Σ^+ is the maximal prime extension of Σ relative to the omitted formula y.' Σ and y are presumed to belong to some language SL_I.

Notation . The expression $\mathbb{C}_{\vdash_{SK3}}(\Delta)$ is used to denote the $SK3$ deductive closure of the set Δ.

Definition 5.2.22. For every $v_{ij} \in \mathbb{V}3$, $\mathbb{D}_{ij}$, *the $SK3$ diagram of v_{ij}*, is defined in the classical way:

$$\{\alpha \in i\} \cup \{\neg\beta | \beta \in j\}$$

We shall use $\mathbb{T}_{ij}$ to stand for $\mathbb{C}_{\vdash_{SK3}}(\mathbb{D}_{ij})$ since it will always be clear from the context that the theories in question are of the $SK3$ flavor.

We see nothing in this of the atomic formulas in I which take the value I, but this is no mistake. In order that the theory of a diagram be able to do its necessary work (in the correspondence theorem for instance) it must be the case that every formula in $\mathbb{T}_{ij}$ be true with respect to v_{ij}. But, as has been pointed out several times, there is no formula of SL_I which is true, relative to an assignment v_{ij}, when α takes the value I relative to v_{ij}. This means that the only method of characterizing 'α takes the value I' in terms of $SK3$ provability by a set, is to say, as we shall do below, that neither α nor $\neg\alpha$ is proved. In other words, whichever formulas are left undecided by $\mathbb{T}_{ij}$ are the ones that take the value I. We should pause for a moment to notice, wryly, that what are doing at this juncture is using something very like what we called 'the truth-value fallacy' in order to represent the third value.

This account of things provides us with a decidedly non-classical curiosity—$\mathbb{T}_{\varnothing\varnothing}$. The diagram $\mathbb{D}_{\varnothing\varnothing}$ is empty, so the corresponding theory contains the $SK3$ consequences of the empty set. Of course there are none so $\mathbb{T}_{\varnothing\varnothing} = \varnothing$.

Before we start presenting results about these theories we shall require the so-called *soundness* of $SK3$ with respect to it's semantics:

Theorem 5.2.23 ($SK3$ **'Soundness' Theorem).** *For every set Γ of formulas and formula α:*
$$\Gamma \vdash \alpha \implies \Gamma \models \alpha$$

Proof. The usual proof can be carried out without difficulty. $\square$

In the classical case and the Ł3 case, we could dispense with the usual proof in favor of a slightly more exotic version which used the correspondence theorem. In this case, the proof of the latter result requires soundness.[19]

The main things to notice about the theories $\mathbb{T}_{ij}$:

Lemma 5.2.24 (First $\mathbb{T}_{ij}$ Lemma). $\mathbb{T}_{ij} \vdash \alpha \implies \|\alpha\|_{ij} = T$

Proof. This follows almost immediately from theorem 5.2.23. For suppose $\mathbb{T}_{ij} \vdash \alpha$. Since $\mathbb{T}_{ij}$ is the closure of $\mathbb{D}_{ij}$, it follows by [T] that $\mathbb{D}_{ij} \vdash \alpha$ and by theorem 5.2.23, $\mathbb{D}_{ij} \models \alpha$. But it is evident that $\left\|\mathbb{D}_{ij}\right\|_{ij} = T$ so it must be the case that $\|\alpha\|_{ij} = T$.
$\square$

Corollary 5.2.25. $\left\|\mathbb{T}_{ij}\right\|_{ij} = T$

---

[19]Which is to say, more properly, that the only proof that we could discover requires that soundness be proved first.

Proof. Since we begin with a set, $\mathbb{D}_{ij}$, all the members of which are true relative to v_{ij} and we add only formulas which are true relative to v_{ij} by the previous lemma, it must be the case that $\mathbb{T}_{ij}$ is true relative to v. $\qquad\square$

Lemma 5.2.26 (Correspondence Lemma for $SK3$). *For every $v_{ij} \in \mathbb{V}3$ and formula α of $SL_{\mathbf{I}}$*

$$\|\alpha\|_{ij} = \left\{ \begin{array}{ll} T & \Longleftrightarrow \quad \mathbb{T}_{ij} \vdash \alpha \\ F & \Longleftrightarrow \quad \mathbb{T}_{ij} \vdash \neg\alpha \\ I & otherwise \end{array} \right.$$

Proof. We use induction on the length of the formula α. In the basis step, α is an atomic formula in $\mathbf{I}$ and the result is trivial on the definition of $\mathbb{D}_{ij}$. In the induction step we have two cases: $\alpha = \beta \vee y$ and $\alpha = \neg\beta$.

$$
\begin{aligned}
\|\beta \vee y\|_{ij} = T \;\; &\Longleftrightarrow\;\; \|\beta\|_{ij} = T \text{ or } \|y\|_{ij} = T \text{ truth-table for } \vee \\
&\Longleftrightarrow\;\; \mathbb{T}_{ij} \vdash \beta \text{ or } \mathbb{T}_{ij} \vdash y \text{ HI} \\
&\Longrightarrow\;\; \mathbb{T}_{ij} \vdash \beta \vee y \text{ by } [\vee\mathbf{I}]. \text{ By lemma 5.2.24} \\
&\Longrightarrow\;\; \|\beta \vee y\|_{ij} = T. \text{ QED}
\end{aligned}
$$

$$
\begin{aligned}
\|\alpha \vee \beta\|_{ij} = F \;\; &\Longleftrightarrow\;\; \|\beta\|_{ij} = F \,\&\, \|y\|_{ij} = F \text{ truth-table for } \vee \\
&\Longleftrightarrow\;\; \mathbb{T}_{ij} \vdash \neg\beta \,\&\, \mathbb{T}_{ij} \vdash \neg y \text{ by HI} \\
&\Longleftrightarrow\;\; \mathbb{T}_{ij} \vdash \neg\beta \wedge \neg y \text{ by } [\wedge] \\
&\Longleftrightarrow\;\; \mathbb{T}_{ij} \vdash \neg(\beta \vee y) \text{ by replacement. QED}
\end{aligned}
$$

In the case in which $\|\beta \vee y\|_{ij} = I$ there is nothing to do since we already know that if and only if T is assigned, $\mathbb{T}_{ij}$ proves the formula, and if and only if F is assigned, the negation of the formula is proved. So if and only if neither one of those values are assigned, neither the formula nor its negation can be proved by $\mathbb{T}_{ij}$.

The negation case holds no surprises.

□

We need this lemma to establish a crucial fact about the theories $\mathbb{T}_{ij}$:

Theorem 5.2.27 ($SK3$ Primeness Theorem). *For every $v_{ij} \in \mathbb{V}3 : PRIME(\mathbb{T}_{ij})$.*

Proof. Suppose $\mathbb{T}_{ij} \vdash \alpha \lor \beta$. Then, by lemma 5.2.24 $\|\alpha \lor \beta\|_{ij} = T$ and, by the truth-table for $\lor$, $\|\alpha\|_{ij} = T$ or $\|\beta\|_{ij} = T$. Thus $\mathbb{T}_{ij} \vdash \alpha$ or $\mathbb{T}_{ij} \vdash \beta$ by the correspondence theorem
.   □

We take over the earlier notion of a *truth-tabular extension* of an assignment v_{ij}, since it is evident that the $SK3$ notion $\|\alpha\|_{ij}$ of the truth-value of a formula of $SL_\mathbf{I}$ relative to an assignment, *is* such an extension.

We use this idea in the same way as before to set up a correspondence between assignments and certain kinds of theories.

The main result is:

Theorem 5.2.28 ($SK3$ Truth-Tabular Extension Theorem).
For every index **I,** *T_{ij} is a truth-tabular extension of v_{ij} (in the sense of $SK3$) provided truth-values are assigned in accord with:*

$$\|\alpha\|_{\mathbb{T}_{ij}} = \begin{cases} T & \Longleftrightarrow & \mathbb{T}_{ij} \vdash \alpha \\ F & \Longleftrightarrow & \mathbb{T}_{ij} \vdash \neg\alpha \\ I & & otherwise \end{cases}$$

Proof. This is one of those arguments with lots of cases. What we have to show is that provability by $\mathbb{T}_{ij}$ obeys the $SK3$ truth-tables.

We begin with the table for disjunction. In that table, a disjunction takes the value T if and only if at least one disjunct takes that value. A translation of this into '$\mathbb{T}_{ij}$

provability-talk' would require that '$\mathbb{T}_{ij} \vdash \alpha \vee \beta$ if and only if $\mathbb{T}_{ij} \vdash \alpha$ or $\mathbb{T}_{ij} \vdash \beta$'. Happily, this is nothing but the requirement of primeness. Next we see that a disjunction takes F if and only if both disjuncts take F. For provability then, we would require that $\mathbb{T}_{ij} \vdash \neg(alpha \vee \beta)$ if and only if $\mathbb{T}_{ij} \vdash \neg\alpha$ and $\mathbb{T}_{ij} \vdash \neg\beta$. The rule of conjunction introduction and a replacement rule suffice to demonstrate this. Finally the table has it that a disjunction takes the value I if and only if both disjuncts take I or one disjunct takes I while the other takes F. This case is a bit messy. To conform to the table it must be the case that $\mathbb{T}_{ij} \nvdash \alpha \vee \beta$ and $\mathbb{T}_{ij} \nvdash \neg(\alpha \vee \beta)$ if and only if (1) $\mathbb{T}_{ij} \nvdash \alpha$ and $\mathbb{T}_{ij} \nvdash \neg\alpha$ and $\mathbb{T}_{ij} \nvdash \beta$ and $\mathbb{T}_{ij} \nvdash \neg\beta$ or (2) ($\mathbb{T}_{ij} \nvdash \alpha$ and $\mathbb{T}_{ij} \nvdash \neg\alpha$ and $\mathbb{T}_{ij} \vdash \neg\beta$)or ($\mathbb{T}_{ij} \nvdash \beta$ and $\mathbb{T}_{ij} \nvdash \neg\beta$ and $\mathbb{T}_{ij} \vdash \neg\alpha$). A bit of concentration may be required to see that $\mathbb{T}_{ij}$ fails to prove both a disjunction and its negation if and only if $\mathbb{T}_{ij}$ fails to prove both disjuncts and at least one of the negations of a disjunct follows from primeness and several rules as well as consistency.

Next the table for negation. In this case we must show first that $\mathbb{T}_{ij} \vdash \neg\alpha$ if and only if $\mathbb{T}_{ij} \vdash \neg\alpha$ which is trivial. Next, for the F case, we need to show that $\mathbb{T}_{ij} \vdash \neg\neg\alpha$ if and only if $T_{ij} \vdash \alpha$ which is a rule of replacement. Finally, for the I case we must show that $\mathbb{T}_{ij} \nvdash \neg\alpha$ and $\mathbb{T}_{ij} \nvdash \neg\neg\alpha$ if and only if $\mathbb{T}_{ij} \nvdash \alpha$ and $\mathbb{T}_{ij} \nvdash \neg\alpha$, which is still trivial.

$\square$

Corollary 5.2.29. *Suppose Δ is a prime SK3 theory, then Δ is a truth-tabular extension (in the sense of SK3) of the assignment $v_{i_\Delta j_\Delta}$ where $i_\Delta = \{\alpha \in \mathbf{I} | \Delta \vdash \alpha\}$ and $j_\Delta = \{\beta \in \mathbf{I} | \Delta \vdash \neg\beta\}$.*

Proof. The proof of this is immediate from the fact that in the previous result, we don't appeal to any special features of $\mathbb{T}_{ij}$ beyond primeness. This result is just another way of saying that every prime $SK3$ theory is some $\mathbb{T}_{ij}$.

☐

Since truth-tabular extensions of assignments v_{ij} are unique we have the following correspondence theorem.

Theorem 5.2.30 ($SK3$ Correspondence Theorem). *For every index* **I** *and formula* α *of* $SL_{\mathbf{I}}$,

$$\|\alpha\|_{ij} = \begin{cases} T & \Longleftrightarrow \mathbb{T}_{ij} \vdash \alpha \\ F & \Longleftrightarrow \mathbb{T}_{ij} \vdash \neg\alpha \\ I & otherwise \end{cases}$$

Proof. This follows immediately from the uniqueness of truth-tabular extensions (providing both are of the same type, of course). ☐

We should take stock of where we are and begin to draw our various bits together into a coherent account of the metalogic of $SK3$.

It has been shown, by defining a construction, that given any set Γ which fails to prove in $SK3$ a formula α, there is some prime theory which includes Γ and also fails to prove α. However, in the definition of $\mathbb{T}_{ij}$, no mention is made of any formula which $\mathbb{T}_{ij}$ fails to prove. The construction obviously results in a member of $\mathbb{T}3$ but can it be shown that every member of $\mathbb{T}3$ can be constructed by the 'omitted formula' construction? In other words: is it the case that for every $\mathbb{T}_{ij} \in \mathbb{T}_{\mathbf{I}}$, there is some set Σ and formula α of $SL_{\mathbf{I}}$, such that $\mathbb{T}_{ij} = \mathbb{M}(\Sigma, \alpha)$? We should hasten to add the condition that $\Sigma \subset \mathbb{T}_{ij}$ to prevent triviality. But even with that proviso, the answer is still that such 'generating' sets and formulas can indeed be found for every member of $\mathbb{T}3$.

One can almost see this in the definition of $\mathbb{T}_{ij}$. By definition this theory is the closure of $\mathbb{D}_{ij}$ so all that remains then is to specify an ordering and an omitted formula.

It turns out that the omitted formula doesn't matter, in the sense that any formula α such that $\mathbb{D}_{ij} \not\vdash \alpha$ and $\mathbb{D}_{ij} \not\vdash \neg\alpha$ can be used. This is established by the following:

Lemma 5.2.31. *For every* $\mathbb{T}_{ij} \in \mathbb{T}3$, *if* α_1 *and* α_2 *are such that* $\mathbb{D}_{ij}$ *proves neither of the formulas and neither of their negations, then*

$$\mathbb{M}(\mathbb{D}ij, \alpha_1) = \mathbb{M}(\mathbb{D}_{ij}, \alpha_2)$$

Proof. We show that for an arbitrary 'excluded' formula α_i, $\mathbb{M}(\mathbb{D}ij, \alpha_i) = \mathbb{C}_{\vdash_{SK3}}(\mathbb{D}_{ij})$.

Since the construction just adds consequences unless a disjunction is added, the two can only differ in that for some $\beta \vee \gamma$ such that $\mathbb{D}_{ij} \vdash \beta \vee \gamma$, $\mathbb{M}(\mathbb{D}_{ij}, \alpha_i)$ contains, say, γ while $Cls(\mathbb{D}_{ij})$ does not. Since the latter set is known to be prime, it must contain the other disjunct, β. But, from the description of the construction on page 96 it can be seen that the only reason for β's omission is that at the stage, say k, where the addition takes place, $\Sigma_{k-1}, \beta \vdash \alpha_i$. We may assume without loss of generality that the construction up to stage k is compatible with $\mathbb{C}_{\vdash_{SK3}}(\mathbb{D}_{ij})$, in other words, that $\Sigma_{k-1} \subseteq \mathbb{T}_{ij}$. But then $\mathbb{T}_{ij}, \beta \vdash \alpha_i$ by [M], $\mathbb{T}_{ij} \vdash \beta$ since $\beta \in \mathbb{T}_{ij}$, so $\mathbb{T}_{ij} \vdash \alpha_i$ by [T]. But now consider the truth-value assignment ν_{ij}. This assignment makes true all of $\mathbb{D}_{ij}$ and gives the value I to all other atomic sentences in $\mathbb{I}$, we know that this assignment makes all of $\mathbb{T}_{ij}$ true and α_i not true. So $\mathbb{T}_{ij} \not\vdash \alpha_i$ which is impossible if $\mathbb{T}_{ij} \vdash \alpha_i$. So $\mathbb{M}(\mathbb{D}_{ij})(\alpha_i, \delta_i)$ cannot differ from $\mathbb{C}_{\vdash_{SK3}}(\mathbb{D}_{ij})$ after all. $\square$

This leaves only the case of a set $\mathbb{T}_{ij} \in \mathbb{T}3$ such that there are no members of $\mathbb{I}$ for which neither the formula nor it's negation is in $\mathbb{D}ij$—those theories for which $i \cup j = \mathbb{I}$. These are the sets which are complete in the classical sense. For sets of this kind there is no excluded formula and we must resort to the somewhat artificial construction $\mathbb{M}(\mathbb{D}_{ij}, \alpha \wedge \neg\alpha)$.

So every $\mathbb{T}_{ij}$ can be constructed by our method, and we have seen already that every prime $SK3$ theory is one of the $\mathbb{T}_{ij}$, so it must follow that we can construct all of the $SK3$ prime theories. It will prove useful to have some notation for the latter class.

Notation . From now on we shall use $\mathbb{T}3_\mathbf{I}$ to refer to the class of proper $SK3$ prime theories built up of formulas of the language $SL_\mathbf{I}$ and also as a predicate indicating membership in that class. When no particular index is at issue we often drop the subscript.

And now these scattered results can be put together.

Theorem 5.2.32 (Equivalence Theorem for $SK3$). *The following are equivalent in $SK3$:*

(1) $\Gamma \vdash \alpha$

(2) $\Gamma \vDash \alpha$

(3) For every $v_{ij} \in \mathbb{V}3 : \|\Gamma\|_{ij} = T \implies \|\alpha\|_{ij} = T$

(4) For every $\mathbb{T}_{ij} \in \mathbb{T}3 : \Gamma \subseteq \mathbb{T}_{ij} \implies \mathbb{T}_{ij} \vdash \alpha$

Proof. The proof resembles the other equivalence results we have seen before, with one crucial difference.

(1) $\implies$ (2). This is just theorem 5.2.23.

(2) $\implies$ (3). This and its converse flow from the fact that this is the definition of $\vDash$.

(3) $\implies$ (4). Both this and its converse follow from the correspondence theorem.

(4) $\implies$ (1). For indirect proof, assume $\Gamma \nvdash \alpha$ (i.e. assume that (1)) is false.

Then by the construction there is some $\Delta = \mathbb{M}(\Gamma, \alpha)$ (which must also be in $\mathbb{T}3_\mathbf{I}$) such that $\Delta \nvdash \alpha$ (i.e. $\neg$ (4)).

We should notice that here too we enjoy the converse of the result, in this case by the grace of [M].

□

What *cannot* be used, even with changes, is the version
of the proof which doesn't use theorem 5.2.23. In that version, which was used for classical sentence logic and in
this chapter for Ł3, there was a proof of equivalence which
showed:

(2) $\iff$ (3)

(3) $\iff$ (4)

(4) $\iff$ (1)

But the proof of the correspondence lemma for $SK3$,
which is used to establish the second equivalence, depends
upon a prior proof that (1) $\implies$ (2) i.e. theorem 5.2.23.

5.3   So How Different are Ł3 and $SK3$?

Towards the beginning of this chapter we suggested that
from a 'laws of thought' perspective the two approaches to
three-valued logic which we treat are as different as different can be.[20] After all, $SK3$ hasn't got any laws of thought
at all.

But there is also an obvious sense in which one might argue that the two are actually the *same* logic. The reason for
such an apparently bizarre assertion is that $\mathbb{T}_I$ and $\mathbb{T}3_I$ are
both isomorphic to $\mathbb{V}3_I$. That these classes are isomorphic
follows from the uniqueness of truth-tabular extensions,
and from the appropriate definition of the notion of a diagram.

What this really means is that each of the logics, in their
own way, can exactly represent all possible distributions
of the (three) truth-values to the members of any index

---

[20]'As alike as chalk and cheese' the old saying has it.

I. But to give the semantics is, in one sense, to provide a distribution of truth-values to atomic sentences; these distributions represent the 'possible worlds' according to the semantics in question.

So 'Both Ł3 and $SK3$ have the same possible worlds' is one way of putting the matter. This is of course not to say that they agree on what formulas are true in each of those worlds. $SK3$ allows that there is a world at which no formula is true, an impossibility for Ł3 which requires that at least the logical truths be true at every world.

5.4 Interpretation Issues

There is a lot of nonsense talked about the interpretation of the values of a many-valued logic, on both the pro-mvl and anti-mvl sides of the fence. One, from the pro side, has already been characterized as 'the truth-value fallacy' but even sillier pronouncements can be found on the other side.

People have said[21] that many-valued logic is *really* two-valued, since either

> the metalanguage is two-valued, or

> everything depends, in the final analysis, upon the true/not true distinction, or

> in every cell of every truth-table, there is a two-valued choice of whether to write a certain value or not.

To which it might be replied

> Whether a logic is such-and-such doesn't typically depend upon whether a metalanguage for that logic is such-and-such. Alternatively, because a logic has a

---

[21]I haven't seen or don't recall anybody saying these things *in print*, but I have heard plenty of people say them.

> metalanguage of a certain kind doesn't mean that it
> fails to have one of another kind.
>
> It isn't clear what sense is to be made of 'everything'
> here. If what is meant is that semantic entailment is
> defined only in terms of truth and untruth, we can
> and should agree. But that certain entailments hold
> and others fail, depends crucially upon the existence
> of other values besides truth and falsehood and the
> behavior of the connectives in terms of those other
> values. As we have seen many times over in this chap-
> ter.
>
> We see your mouth opening and closing but all we
> hear is 'blah blah blah.'

Nevertheless this kind of thinking can be made into something less silly, just as the truth-value fallacy can be used
at the meta-level to do something useful.

In a series of papers (Scott, 1973, 1974) Dana Scott has
suggested a way of interpreting the values of Łukasiewicz
and several other many-valued logics, in terms of sets of
(indexed) two-valued valuations. Scott floated this technique as a way of avoiding the mysterious (to him) idea
of *designated* truth-values.

This concept is required in the context of numerical values in order to indicate which of them are 'the good guys.'
For example, if one were to do three-valued logic using 1,
2, and 3 to stand for the values, it wouldn't be clear until
it was stipulated, which values were to count in defining
semantic entailment. The stipulation in question is generally framed by saying, for example, that the value 1 is
designated. From that point on, we know that semantic
entailment is to be defined by saying that it holds exactly
when, if the premises all take the value 1 relative to an assignment v, then so does the conclusion.

From his remarks in (Scott, 1973) it seems that Scott finds this usage objectionable because it is not phrased in terms of the 'real' truth-values, truth and falsehood, hence his revisionist program of interpretation. A disinterested observer might remark, however, that Scott's requirement that the 'non-standard' values be represented as sets of indexed (two-valued) truth-value assignments is just as mysterious. All that has happened is that the locus of mystery has changed to the indices of the assignments and Scott's attempt to provide an interpretation of these indices is no more successful than others (Łukasiewicz's for instance) attempts to interpret the non-standard values *directly*.

To some extent our presentation has side-stepped these issues since it was stipulated (in as loud a voice as possible) that our set of truth-values is a superset of the classical set. But the issues cannot be ignored forever. Several people have suggested a program which involves the designation of more than one value. In the case of three valued logic, this would come down to allowing the value I as well as the value T to be *truth-like*. Does such a suggestion make any sense at all? The answer to this is 'yes and no.'

It is surely sensible to distinguish between those contexts in which the main concern is to ward against accepting as true something untrue, and those in which the concern is rather to avoid rejecting as untrue, something true. Something of this sort accounts for the distinction between type I and type II tests in the discipline of statistical hypothesis testing. However, such distinctions are clearly context dependent and aren't very sensible absent a reference to contexts.

We shall formalize a system which is inspired by these considerations. Given the bits and pieces of background motivation, such a system must make provision for contexts and also for some method of *projecting* or perhaps *collapsing* three values into two. The method by which all

this will be accomplished requires adding three new connectives to the object language, and using two distinct va-
rieties of truth-value assignment as well as items intended
to represent contexts, in the semantical metalanguage.

There are two new things in the object language. The
first is a unary operator which will be represented by ϕ. It
is informally interpreted as a *truth*-operator, so that $\phi(\alpha)$
will be read 'It is ϕ-true that α' (parentheses will be dropped
when no confusion will result). It is this sort of expression which will allow us to give a two-valued account of the
three-valued logic. We also add a zero-ary operator (which
is to say constant-valued sentence), represented by ✠. The
constant does not lie within the scope of ϕ. In other words,
expressions like $\phi\alpha$ are not regarded as well-formed whenever α contains the symbol ✠. In keeping with this, the
constant will be regarded as part of the primary language
only, which is to say that it will not fall within range of the
secondary truth-value apparatus defined just below. We
shall refer to the expanded langauge as *BSL* and when, as
usual, we confine the atomic sentences of our language to
a so-called *index* **I**, the language will be indicated by BSL_I.

ϕ was referred to as a truth-operator just now, and by
this is meant that it satisfies the conditions found in our
earlier encounter with the concept on page 58.

Definition 5.4.1. A *bi-semantic evaluation E* for a
language BSL_I is defined to be a triple $(i, \langle j, k \rangle, cxt)$
where $i \subseteq$ **I** represents the *primary truth-value
assignment* (of *E*), j and k are disjoint subsets of **I** the
pair of which represent the *secondary truth-value
assignment* (of *E*) and cxt, the *context* (of *E*), is either l
or c.

We shall have reason to deploy this idea later in this volume, which explains why we present things as we have.

Notation . We use $\mathbb{E}$ to refer to the class of bi-semantic evaluations.

Notation . £ for '¬✠'

We define the notion of (secondary) truth-value relative to the bi-semantic evaluation E:

Definition 5.4.2. $\|P\|_E$, the secondary truth-value relative to the bi-semantic evaluation E, is defined inductively:

$$\|\alpha\|_E = \begin{cases} T \iff \alpha \in j \\ F \iff \alpha \in k \\ I \text{ otherwise} \end{cases}$$

If α is a classical compound, then $\|alpha\|_E$ is computed via the strong tables (see pages 70-75).

If $\alpha = \phi(\beta)$ then $\|\alpha\|_E = \|\beta\|_E$. This is referred to as the *transparency* condition on ϕ.

And finally, the reason for all this:

Definition 5.4.3. The predicate 'The formula α is true relative to the primary truth-value assignment of E', written $\vDash_E \alpha$, is defined inductively

If $\alpha \in \mathbf{I}$ then $\vDash_E \alpha \iff \alpha \in i$.

If α is a classical compound then the usual classical truth-conditions apply.

If $\alpha = ✠$ then $\vDash_E \alpha$ if and only if the context of E is c.

If $\alpha = \phi\beta$ then

$$\vDash_E \alpha \iff \begin{cases} \|\beta\|_E = T \text{ if the context of } E \text{ is } c \\ \|\beta\|_E \neq F \text{ if the context of } E \text{ is } l \end{cases}$$

From this definition the usual accounts of (bi-)semantic entailment and logical truth follow at once. We shall refer to the *logic* which consists of all those pairs (Γ, α) such that $\Gamma \vDash \alpha$, by means of $B3$.

The context tags l and c are meant to suggest 'liberal' and 'conservative.' The ϕ operator just introduced lies in the middle of the range of permissible operators, as regards it's distribution properties. It's relatively easy to see that

$\phi(\alpha \wedge \beta) \equiv (\phi\alpha \wedge \phi\beta)$, and

$\phi(\alpha \vee \beta) \equiv (\phi\alpha \vee \phi\beta)$ are both logically true in $B3$, or alternatively that

$[\phi\wedge] \ \phi(\alpha \wedge \beta) \longleftrightarrow (\phi\alpha \wedge \phi\beta)$ and

$[\phi\vee] \ \phi(\alpha \vee \beta) \longleftrightarrow (\phi\alpha \vee \phi\beta)$ are both correct replacement rules for $B3$.

Suppose now that $\|\alpha\|_E = I$ and $\|\beta\|_E = F$ for some bi-semantic evaluation E, the context of which is l. It is easy to see that since $\|\alpha \supset \beta\|_E = I$, $\vDash_E \phi(\alpha \supset \beta)$. On the other hand, since $\vDash_E \phi\alpha$ and $\nvDash_E \phi\beta$, $\nvDash_E \phi\alpha \supset \phi\beta$. So ϕ fails to strongly distribute over $\supset$.

Keeping this same case, it is clear that $\|\neg\alpha\|_E = I$ so $\vDash_E \phi\neg\alpha$. But since $\vDash_E \phi\alpha$, $\nvDash_E \neg\phi\alpha$. So ϕ does not distribute strongly over $\neg$.

On the other hand we do have some partial distribution results. When the context of E is c, then both

$\models_E \phi \neg \alpha \supset \neg \phi \alpha$ and

$\models_E \phi(\alpha \supset \beta) \supset (\phi \alpha \supset \phi \beta)$

while if the context of E is l then both

$\models_E \neg \phi \alpha \supset \phi \neg \alpha$ and

$\models_E (\phi \alpha \supset \phi \beta) \supset \phi(\alpha \supset \beta)$

As for the other requirements on truth-operators, the issue of idempotency is easily seen to be settled by the transparency condition, which collapses the secondary truth-value of both $\phi \alpha$ and $\phi \phi \alpha$ into the secondary value of α, for every evaluation E.

On the duality condition, we first issue a definition in aid of brevity.

Definition 5.4.4. Define $\psi \alpha$ to be the formula $\neg \phi \neg \alpha$.

It is easily checked that ψ 'reverses c and l', in the sense that:

If the context of E is l then $\models_E \psi \alpha \iff \|\alpha\|_E = T$ and

If the context of E is C then $\models_E \psi \alpha \iff \|\alpha\|_E \neq F$

It is similarly easy to check that ψ strongly distributes over both $\vee$ and $\wedge$, and that $\psi \psi \alpha \longleftrightarrow \psi \alpha$. From all this it follows that ϕ (and ψ as well) satisfies the duality requirement.

There is one more requirement, perhaps the most controversial, which one could apply to truth-operators. If ϕ is supposed to formalize some or other recognizable notion of truth, then the relation defined by

$$\phi[\Gamma] \models \phi \alpha$$

should be recognizable as an inference relation. It says, after all, that the truth (in the ϕ sense) of the premises, Γ implies the truth (in the ϕ sense) of the conclusion α, and what is that if not inference (from the semantic perspective)?

At least part of the controversy[22] comes in when one attempts to specify what the minimum requirements are for some relation to be an inference relation. We shall take the initial position[23] that at least the three structural rules [R], [M], and [T] must hold for the candidate relation. From an earlier result, on page 61, we know that this kind of relation must satisfy [R],[M], and [T], because classical provability does.

5.5   Proof theory and Metalogic of $B3$

We have already announced much of the proof-theory of $B3$ although it was scattered through the previous section. Here it is, gathered together, and with a few new items.

Classical Principles

For the classical portion of $B3$, i.e. that fragment which doesn't mention ϕ, ✠, or £, the usual classical principles apply.

'Political' Principles

$\Gamma \vdash £ \vee$ ✠

$\Gamma \vdash £ \supset (\psi\alpha \supset \phi\alpha)$

$\Gamma \vdash$ ✠ $\supset (\phi\alpha \supset \psi\alpha)$

---

[22]Another part of the controversy would be posed by those who don't think that inference can (or at least should) be construed semantically.

[23]Once we have given the matter some thought, we might choose to relax the requirement that [R] and [M] hold unrestrictedly.

'Truth' Principles

$$\phi(\alpha \wedge \beta) \longleftrightarrow \phi\alpha \wedge \phi\beta$$

$$\phi(\alpha \vee \beta) \longleftrightarrow \phi\alpha \vee \phi\beta$$

$$\psi(\alpha \wedge \beta) \longleftrightarrow \psi\alpha \wedge \psi\beta$$

$$\psi(\alpha \vee \beta) \longleftrightarrow \psi\alpha \vee \psi\beta$$

$$\vdash \alpha \equiv \beta \implies \vdash \phi\alpha \equiv \phi\beta$$

$$\vdash \alpha \equiv \beta \implies \vdash \psi\alpha \equiv \psi\beta$$

In the following ζ is any finite string consisting of zero or more occurrences of ϕ, and ψ, and zero or an even number of occurrences of $\neg$.

$$\psi\alpha \longleftrightarrow \psi\zeta\alpha$$

$$\phi\alpha \longleftrightarrow \phi\zeta\alpha$$

$$\psi\neg\alpha \longleftrightarrow \psi\neg\zeta\alpha$$

$$\phi\neg\alpha \longleftrightarrow \phi\neg\zeta\alpha$$

Our metatheory will employ the notion of a diagram which we have already used to good effect in other contexts. In the present context it comes out like:

Definition 5.5.1. Let E be a bi-semantic evaluation of a language BSL_I for which the context is c. The *diagram of E* indicated by $\mathbb{D}_E$, is defined

$$\mathbb{D}_E = \left\{ \begin{array}{l} \{\alpha_1 \in i\} \cup \{\neg\alpha_2 | \alpha_2 \in \mathbf{I} \,\&\, \alpha_2 \notin i\} \\ \cup \{\phi(\alpha_3) | \alpha_3 \in j\} \cup \{\phi(\neg\alpha_4) | \alpha_4 \in k\} \\ \cup \{\psi(\alpha_5) \wedge \psi(\neg\alpha_5) | \alpha_5 \in \mathbf{I} \,\&\, \alpha_5 \notin j \,\&\, \alpha_5 \notin k\} \\ \cup \{\maltese\} \end{array} \right.$$

Let E be a bi-semantic evaluation of a language BSL_I for which the context is l. The *diagram of E* is defined

$$\mathbb{D}_E = \left\{ \begin{array}{l} \{\alpha_1 \in i\} \cup \{\neg\alpha_2 | \alpha_2 \in \mathbf{I} \,\&\, \alpha_2 \notin i\} \\ \cup \{\psi(\alpha_3) | \alpha_3 \in j\} \cup \{\psi(\neg\alpha_4) | \alpha_4 \in k\} \\ \cup \{\phi(\alpha_5) \wedge \phi(\neg\alpha_5) | \alpha_5 \in \mathbf{I} \,\&\, \alpha_5 \notin j \,\&\, \alpha_5 \notin k\} \\ \cup \{\pounds\} \end{array} \right.$$

Given a diagram $\mathbb{D}_E$ we shall refer to its $B3$ deductive closure by means of $\mathbb{T}_E$, while the entire class of such theories for a given index will be represented by $\mathbb{T}_{\mathbb{E}}$. It will turn out that these theories have all the properties that we need and expect.

The main thing to worry about in matching $\mathbb{T}_E$ with $\vDash_E$ is whether or not the former has the secondary assignment right. This is a matter, since the secondary assignment is a truth-tabular extension of the secondary truth-value assignment, of showing that $\mathbb{T}_E$'s translation of taking on the secondary truth-values obeys the strong tables.

Lemma 5.5.2 (The $\|.\|_{\mathbb{T}_E}$ Lemma). *For every bi-semantic evaluation E of a language BSL_I and formula α the following truth-value distribution schemes are truth-tabular extensions (in the correct sense)*

If the context of E is l

$$\|\alpha\|_{\mathbb{T}_E} = \left\{ \begin{array}{l} T \iff \mathbb{T}_E \vdash \psi\alpha \\ F \iff \mathbb{T}_E \vdash \psi\neg\alpha \\ I \iff \mathbb{T}_E \vdash \phi\alpha \,\&\, \mathbb{T}_E \vdash \phi\neg\alpha \end{array} \right.$$

If the context of E is c

$$\|\alpha\|_{\mathbb{T}_E} = \begin{cases} T & \Longleftrightarrow & \mathbb{T}_E \vdash \phi\alpha \\ F & \Longleftrightarrow & \mathbb{T}_E \vdash \phi\neg\alpha \\ I & \Longleftrightarrow & \mathbb{T}_E \vdash \psi\alpha \,\&\, \mathbb{T}_E \vdash \psi\neg\alpha \end{cases}$$

Proof. We have lots of cases. Start with a conjunction $\alpha \wedge \beta$ and context c. We have to show that:

$(\wedge T)$ $\mathbb{T}_E \vdash \phi(\alpha \wedge \beta) \iff \mathbb{T}_E \vdash \alpha \,\&\, \mathbb{T}_E \vdash \beta$

$(\wedge F)$ $\mathbb{T}_E \vdash \phi(\neg(\alpha \wedge \beta)) \iff \mathbb{T}_E \vdash \phi(\neg\alpha)$ or $\mathbb{T}_E \vdash \phi(\neg\beta)$

$(\wedge I)$ $\mathbb{T}_E \vdash \psi(\alpha \wedge \beta) \,\&$
$\quad\quad \mathbb{T}_E \vdash \psi(\neg(\alpha \wedge \beta)) \iff$

(1) $\mathbb{T}_E \vdash \psi(\alpha) \,\&\, \mathbb{T}_E \vdash \psi(\neg\alpha) \,\&\, \mathbb{T}_E \vdash \psi(\beta)$
$\quad \,\&\, \mathbb{T}_E \vdash \psi(\neg\beta)$ or

(2) $\mathbb{T}_E \vdash \phi(\alpha) \,\&\, \mathbb{T}_E \vdash \psi(\beta) \,\&\, \mathbb{T}_E \vdash \psi(\neg\beta)$ or

(3) $\mathbb{T}_E \vdash \phi(\beta) \,\&\, \mathbb{T}_E \vdash \psi(\alpha) \,\&\, \mathbb{T}_E \vdash \psi(\neg\alpha)$

The first case follows at once from the conjunction rule and the distribution of ϕ, while the second follows from the extensionality of ϕ together with the fact that $\mathbb{T}_E$ is prime. Only the third case requires some effort, but hardly an Herculean amount.

Since $\mathbb{T}_E \vdash \maltese$, $\mathbb{T}_E \vdash \phi\alpha \supset \psi\alpha$, for every formula α by one of the political principles. It follows that each of (1), (2), and (3) imply that
(4) $\psi(\beta \wedge \gamma) \wedge \psi(\neg(\beta \wedge \gamma))$
Thus, by classical reasoning and the conjunction rule, $\mathbb{T}_E \vdash \psi(\alpha \wedge \beta) \,\&\, \mathbb{T}_E \vdash \psi(\neg(\alpha \wedge \beta))$ also.

Next assume that $\mathbb{T}_E \vdash$ (4). By classical reasoning together with truth principles this amounts to $\mathbb{T}_E \vdash (\psi(\beta \wedge \gamma) \wedge \psi\neg\beta) \vee (\psi(\beta \wedge \gamma) \wedge \psi\neg\gamma)$. Since $\mathbb{T}_E$ is prime it must prove one or the other disjunct. Assume that $\mathbb{T}_E \vdash \psi(\beta \wedge \gamma) \wedge \psi\neg\beta$. If $\mathbb{T}_E \vdash \psi\neg\gamma$, then $\mathbb{T}_E \vdash$ (3), while if $\mathbb{T}_E \nvdash \psi\neg\gamma$, then by maximality of $\mathbb{T}_E \vdash \neg\psi\neg\gamma$ which is to say that $\mathbb{T}_E \vdash \phi\gamma$, and thus $\mathbb{T}_E$ proves (1). In either case then, $\mathbb{T}_E$ proves the disjunction since it proves a disjunct. If $\mathbb{T}_E \vdash (\psi(\beta \wedge \gamma) \wedge \psi\neg\gamma)$ then similar reasoning shows that once again $\mathbb{T}_E$ proves the entire disjunction by virtue of proving a disjunct. So by classical reasoning, $\mathbb{T}_E$ proves the disjunction. QED

Next, for context c, consider a negation, $\neg\alpha$. We must show

$(\neg T)$ $\mathbb{T}_E \vdash \phi(\neg\alpha) \iff \mathbb{T}_E \vdash \phi(\neg\alpha)$

$(\neg F)$ $\mathbb{T}_E \vdash \phi(\neg\neg\alpha) \iff \mathbb{T}_E \vdash \phi(\alpha)$

$(\neg I)$ $\mathbb{T}_E \vdash \psi(\neg\alpha) \ \& \ \mathbb{T}_E \vdash \psi(\neg\neg\alpha) \iff \mathbb{T}_E \vdash \psi(\alpha) \ \& \ \mathbb{T}_E \vdash \psi(\neg\alpha)$

Each of these cases is trivial although the final two require the double negation elimination replacement rule.

Finally, for context c, we consider the case of a ϕ formula, say $\phi(\alpha)$. The transparency requirement is that $\phi(\alpha)$ take on whatever value α takes on (relative to the secondary assignment). In other words what needs to be shown is

(ϕT) $\mathbb{T}_E \vdash \phi(\phi(\alpha)) \iff \mathbb{T}_E \vdash \phi(\alpha)$

(ϕF) $\mathbb{T}_E \vdash \phi\neg(\phi(\alpha)) \iff \mathbb{T}_E \vdash \phi(\neg\alpha)$

(ϕI) $\mathbb{T}_E \vdash \psi(\phi\alpha) \ \& \ \mathbb{T}_E \vdash \psi(\neg\phi\alpha) \iff \mathbb{T}_E \vdash \psi(\alpha) \ \& \ \mathbb{T}_E \vdash \psi(\neg\alpha)$

The first of these is just the idempotence of ϕ while the second follows from the equivalence of $\phi\psi(\neg\alpha)$ with $\phi(\neg\alpha)$, which is one of the 'truth' principles. For the final case, the same group of truth principles together with the idempotence of ψ does the trick.

We must do all this again for context l, but each of the above arguments will go through interchanging ϕ with ψ.

$\square$

We already know from our experience of classical met-alogic that $\mathbb{T}_E \vdash$ is a truth-functional extension of the primary truth-value assignment. which is to say that the following result is immediate from the uniqueness of truth-functional, and truth-tabular extensions:

Theorem 5.5.3 (Correspondence Theorem for $B3$). *For every bi-semantic evaluation of a language BSL_1 and every formula α of that language:* $\mathbb{T}_E \vdash \alpha \iff \vDash_E \alpha$

Theorem 5.5.4 (Equivalence Theorem for $B3$). *Given a language BSL_1 with Γ and α a set of formulas of that language and a formula of that language, respectively, the following are equivalent for the logic $B3$:*

(1) $\Gamma \vdash \alpha$

(2) $\Gamma \vDash \alpha$

(3) For every $E \in \mathbb{E_I}$, $\vDash_E \Gamma \implies \vDash_E \alpha$

(4) For every $\mathbb{T}_E \in \mathbb{T_E}$, $\Gamma \subseteq \Delta \implies \Delta \vdash \alpha$

Proof. Our previous classical arguments can be recycled except when we wish to show that (3) and (4) are equivalent in which case we must use our new correspondence theorem. □

Theorem 5.5.5 (Isomorphism Theorem for $B3$). *For every index* I: $\mathbb{T_E}$ *and* $\mathbb{E}$ *are isomorphic*

5.6 The Interpretation Problem Again

Earlier, we spoke of the difficulty of finding compelling interpretations for statements like 'α takes the value I.' It is time to revisit this issue. We can see that bi-semantics provides an answer to Scott's worries about the concept of designation.

But is that enough to solve any remaining issues about the meaning of the non-classical truth-values?[24] It isn't clear that we can claim to have fully put to rest all and any worries about the interpretation of the non-classical values. But it also isn't entirely clear (to me at least) that all the questions about the interpretation of the *classical* values have been answered either. What I do feel comfortable saying is that a contribution has been made to the debate.

That contribution might be put this way: bi-semantics allows us to interpret the value I, for instance, in a classical way by saying that (relative to the appropriate semantic structure) assigning the value I to α means that $\phi\alpha$ is true (if the context is liberal) or that $\phi\alpha$ is false (if the context is conservative). Of course that leaves unanswered the obvious question 'What does $\phi\alpha$ mean?' Haven't we simply pushed the problem into a different corner—committing precisely the sin which was earlier attributed to Scott?

The way out is to provide an interpretation for ϕP, and this is going to be a bit slippery. The earlier formulation 'α is ϕ-true' won't be very useful except at the very highest level of abstraction. Below that, for particular applications of bi-semantics, I suggest that ϕ will represent some species of 'acceptable,' something less sweeping than full frontal metaphysical truth, but still recognizable as a worth-while property.[25]

5.7   Beyond Three Values

Once we leave the relative security of three-valued logic, we find ourselves on a slippery slope. What is the 'next step?' There isn't very much to choose, on theoretical grounds at

---

[24]This is not to say that I have actually checked with Scott concerning the proposed answer to his question. I have not.

[25]In chapter 6 we try a more detailed interpretation along the lines of "It would be reasonable to accept...."

least, between four values, five values, ..., any finite number of values.[26]

In other words, we quickly find ourselves with an infinite number of values, indeed the traditional set of values in this case is the closed unit interval $[0, 1]$. Apart from the extreme values 0 (false) and 1 (true),[27] the other values are represented by rationals such as $\frac{1}{2}$ $\frac{2}{3}$ and the like.[28]

In this context we are clearly not able to use truth-tables to present the connectives and are required to employ functions instead—which we might call the *associated* functions. For example the following provide a way of uniquely extending any infinite valued truth-value assignment v to all formulas of the infinite valued Łukasiewicz logic, which is called Ł$_\omega$:

$$\|\alpha\|_v = v(\alpha) \text{ if } \alpha \text{ is an atomic formula}$$

$$\|\alpha \wedge \beta\|_v = \min(\|\alpha\|_v, \|\beta\|_v)$$

$$\|\alpha \vee \beta\|_v = \max(\|\alpha\|_v, \|\beta\|_v)$$

$$\|\neg\alpha\|_v = 1 - \|\alpha\|_v$$

$$\|\alpha \supset \beta\|_v = \min(1, 1 - (\|\alpha\|_v + \|\beta\|_v))$$

At first flush, this all looks very manageable. In fact these definitions make no reference to any number of values and, as is easily checked, give us the Ł3-tables for 3 values. But when the number of values transcends the finite, something very different happens.

---

[26]This is a trifle brisk. Historically, some have thought of four-valued logic as a natural vehicle for doing modal logic. Łukasiewicz and Rosser and Turquette, in particular.

[27]Though Scott Scott (1973) has suggested an interpretation in which these values represent degrees of error. Under that interpretation 0 would mean 'no-error' and so would play the part of 'true.'

[28]It can be shown that using only the rational values in the unit interval and ignoring the irrational ones has no logical effect, but only, as one might say, a topological effect, at least until we introduce quantifiers.

To see this, consider the 'overline' negation introduced for Ł3. In other words, the defined connective:

$$\bar{\alpha} \text{ for } \alpha \supset \neg\alpha$$

While this notation works well for Ł3, it becomes rather cumbersome for Ł4, Ł5, ... For this reason we shall change to the notation $N(\alpha)$ when we iterate the conditional connective into an ever expanding nest. In other words,

$$N^2(\alpha) \text{ for } \alpha \supset (\alpha \supset \neg\alpha)$$

This does for Ł4, what $\bar{\alpha}$ does for Ł3, which is to say that it provides a two-valued species of negation for the former logic. And that's what $N^3(\alpha)$ does for 5-valued logic and so on. So for k-valued logic (of the Łukasiewicz sort) we would require $N^{k-2}(\alpha)$ to effect the same purpose.

With a bit of fiddling we can easily derive the associated function:

$$\|N^n(\alpha)\| = \min(1, 1 - \|\alpha\| + n(1 - \|\alpha\|))$$

The function is all very well for any finite number of values but nothing will perform this valuable service for infinite valued logic. This, one might suppose, is bad enough, but there is worse news just over the horizon.

First, let us represent the graph of the function $N^n(\alpha)$ as in figure 5.1.

Next we define the set $\Sigma(\alpha)$ to be the smallest set which contains the sequence

$$\bar{\bar{\alpha}}, \overline{N^2(\alpha)}, \overline{N^3(\alpha)}, \overline{N^4(\alpha)}, \dots$$

Lemma 5.7.1. *For any (infinite-valued) truth-value assignment v, and any formula α, if $\|\alpha\|_v < 1$ then there is some integer k such that $\left\|N^k(\alpha)\right\|_v = 1$.*

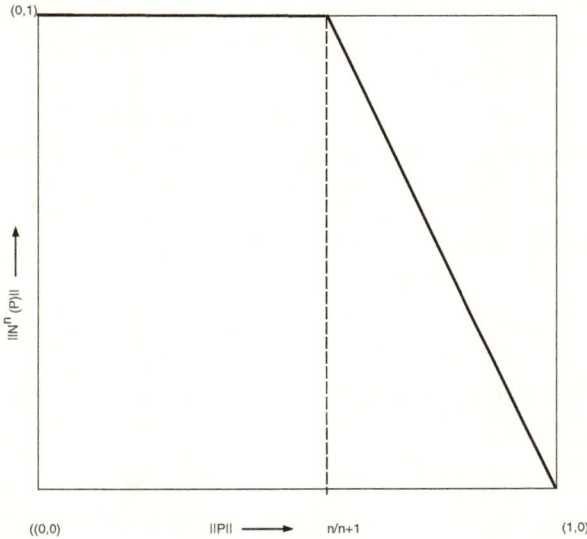

Figure 5.1: Graph of the N-function

Proof. The proof is immediate. By examining figure 5.1 we see that we can simply take the least k such that $\|\alpha\|_v \leq \frac{k}{k+1}$. $\square$

Corollary 5.7.2. $\Sigma(\alpha) \vDash_{Ł_\omega} \alpha$

Proof. From the lemma we know that any formula α which takes a value less than 1 (relative to an assignment v) will have some 'N-negation' which takes 1 (relative to v). But the bar-negation of that N-negation belongs to the sequence $\Sigma(\alpha)$ by definition and the bar-negation of the value 1, is 0. So it is impossible to find any assignment relative to which all the members of $\Sigma(\alpha)$ take the value 1 while α takes any value less than 1. $\square$

Now for the bad news.

Theorem 5.7.3. *$Ł_\omega$ is non-compact.*

Proof. This follows at once from the observation that if $\Sigma^*(\alpha)$ is any finite subset of $\Sigma(\alpha)$, then $\Sigma^*(\alpha) \not\models \alpha$. For if $\Sigma^*(\alpha)$ is finite, there must be some integer j such that $\overline{N^i(\alpha)} \in \Sigma^*(\alpha) \implies i \leq j$. In this case we simply select any infinite-valued assignment v with the property that $\frac{j}{j+1} < \|\alpha\|_v < 1$ and such that $\left\|N^j(\alpha)\right\|_v \leq \frac{1}{2}$. It follows from the definition of $\left\|N^k(\alpha)\right\|$ that

$$\overline{N^k(\alpha)} \in \Sigma^*(P) \implies \left\|N^k(\alpha)\right\|_v \leq \frac{1}{2}$$

and hence that every member of $\Sigma^*(\alpha)$ takes the value 1 relative to v.   □

To put the matter in somewhat less technical language: entailment in $Ł_\omega$ is essentially infinitary—there are infinite premise sets which entail certain conclusions even though no finite subset does. Before we shrug this off with a 'What would you expect from infinite-valued logic?' we should remind ourselves that the proof theory doesn't work this way. Since we require that proofs be finite sequences, it just cannot be the case that some set proves a conclusion without a finite subset also enjoying this property. It follows then that we cannot prove for $Ł_\omega$, that entailment is equivalent to provability.

Part Two:
An Application of Modal and Many-Valued Logics

Six

Epistemic Logic

6.1 Introduction

In this chapter[1] we begin to examine the possibility of applying logic to epistemology. This kind of application first sprang into prominence in the 20th Century with the publication of Hintikka's book (Hintikka, 1962). In that book 'the' logic of knowledge, is pursued by essentially semantic means. We are invited to notice that 'a knows that α' is true (relative to some context c) if and only if α belongs to every set of sentences which is consistent with everything that a knows. Such a set, which might also be characterized as a set of sentences which are true, *for all that a knows*, is called one of a's *epistemic alternatives* (relative to the context c).

One can obtain a truth-condition, by allowing that the contexts with respect to which a is said to know that α or otherwise, are the same objects which respect to which

---

[1]Much of the material in this chapter began life as a reprise of material first presented in (?). However it soon became clear that the initial approach suffered numerous infelicities (to put the matter charitably) and it seemed best to rework the entire thing. Thus was born (Schotch, 2000). This chapter is an expansion and further reworking.

other sentences take on truth-values. Having done that, all that needs doing is to determine the properties of the relation of epistemic alternativeness. As Hintikka defines this relation it is reflexive and transitive. It follows that the logic of 'epistemic necessity'—viz. '*a* knows that *α*', is that normal modal logic known as S4.

There are several problems with this approach.

1. Epistemologists, many of them at least, think that they already know the truth-condition for '*a* knows that *α*' or at least something close. The Hintikka condition isn't even close.

2. Already established researchers might be willing to take up a new formalism, if it seemed to offer advantages in dealing with an existing problem. But epistemic logic seems to be made of the whole cloth. In other words, epistemic logic seems most inviting to researchers in epistemic logic, rather than other disciplines.

3. It isn't hard to see that '*a* knows that *α*' will be true on the Hintikka account whenever *α* is entailed by what *a* knows. But even the Stoic sage is not required to know all the consequences of whatever she knows.

4. Since the relation of epistemic alternativeness is transitive on the Hintikka account[2] it will turn out to be the case that '*a* knows that *α*' must obey the characteristic law of S4 which is, in epistemic form: 'If *a* knows that *α*, then *a* knows that *a* knows that *α*.' (This principle was dubbed KK). It is far from clear however that KK is correct on any of the established theories of what it means for *a* to know something.

---

[2]and on any account which like Hintikka's, interprets the relation as set inclusion

5. On the Hintikka approach there will turn out to be logical truths of the form '*a* knows that *α*,' but this is absurd. *a* might know something *α* as a matter of logic—if *a* has done, or at least seen, the proof of *α*, for example. But to assert that '*a* knows that *α*' might itself be provable, in the absence of any information about *a*, (the language *a* speaks, the evidence, if any, that *a* has as regards the matter at hand, or what *a* believes), is simply crazy. It cannot and should not be a truth of logic that anybody knows anything. We shall say below that Hintikka has offended the principle of *the contingency of knowledge.*

Of these, the most persistent criticism of Hintikka's approach, in print at least, has been 3—which has come to be called the problem (for Hintikka) of *logical omniscience,* followed closely by 4. There has been to-ing and fro-ing over the omniscience issue, and some fairly loose talk about 'ideal knowers,' but it rankles the naive and the cognoscenti alike. A dispassionate observer might hold that 3 and 5 are each decisive against Hintikka. Whether or not the judgement of history is dispassionate, it seems to have gone solidly against Hintikka, at least as far as converting any mainstream epistemologists to his cause.[3] For this reason it seems a useful strategy to restructure the whole approach attempting to take into account as many of the criticisms as possible.

The objections characterized above as decisive are arguments against *normality* in the sense that they would stand against any attempt to pass off a normal modal logic as an epistemic logic. In view of this, the logic won't be normal.

---

[3]This is not to say that there is currently no interest in epistemic logic. Apart from specialists, there has arisen a class of researchers who are examining a possible role for epistemic logic in 'knowledge representation'—an emerging area in cognitive science. See e.g. (Thijsse, 1992)

In fact, given 5, it must be what we might call *strongly* non-normal.[4]

But before we seize the bit between our teeth and rush off to construct a logic, let's first find something for the logic to do. In this way we hope to forestall objection 2. It won't be enough to say that we are investigating the logic of knowledge or belief without having some answer to the question 'So what?' or worse, 'Who cares?' Since inference is the soul of logic, this leads to asking which inferences are the important ones in epistemology. There are lots of candidates fortunately, but perhaps the most central, at least historically, are those inferences surrounding the position of the skeptic. We make that the focus of our logical attention.

Since ancient of days, the skeptic has been a thorn in our sides. But before we move against her, let us remind ourselves that thorns can play an important part in the scheme of things. For this reason we shall not take the skeptical position lightly, though we end up attacking it, in a certain sense. We shall do that by formulating an account of '*a* knows that ...' on which the skeptical argument is invalid. But in carrying out this program, we shall attempt to make our formal proposal as palatable as possible to the skeptic. It will turn out to be quite surprising how palatable that is.

The Skeptical Argument

What happens when we argue with the skeptic? We say: 'There is a table before us.' And she replies 'But if you were so many brains in so many vats, there wouldn't be a table before you, would there? There would only be the vats.' To which we charitably respond: 'That would be true enough, *if* we were brains in vats—but we are not. At the very worst,

---

[4]According to this usage a modal logic is strongly non-normal if and only if for every formula α, $\nvdash \Box\alpha$.

we are brains in heads.' It seems we have played into her hands by taking such a tack. 'Ah' she says 'but you don't *know* that you aren't brains in vats since if you were, you might have exactly the sensations you now have! It follows that you do not know that there is a table before you.'

We have fallen for one of the oldest tricks in the book— misdirection. Incensed by the outlandish idea that we might be brains in vats without knowing it, we seize on that part of the argument and attempt to wrestle it to the ground. In our rage, we commit the worst excesses of ordinary language philosophy and talk endlessly about what we mean by evidence, and how we distinguish between real and apparent. Or we get out our philosophy of science and excoriate the skeptical hypothesis for it's lack of modesty, conservatism, or any other virtue. Throughout all of this, the skeptic nods wisely and offers only an occasional 'Quite right, too!' to encourage us in our folly. Neither ordinary language, nor the scientific viewpoint, are going to save us from the skeptic.

Let's not fall into this trap, as so many have before us. Instead, let's take a closer look at the argument, and not worry about outrageous possibilities. In it's most general form, it goes like this where α represents some homely empirical claim, and H the outlandish skeptical hypothesis:

M-version

1. $\alpha \supset \neg H$ (e.g. If there is a table before you, then you aren't a brain in a vat (BIAV).)

2. $K\alpha \supset K\neg H$ (e.g. If you know that there is a table before you, then you know that you aren't a BIAV.)

3. $\neg K\neg H$ (e.g. You do not know that you aren't a BIAV) therefore, by *modus tollens*:

4. $\neg K\alpha$ (e.g. You don't know that there is a table before you.

The name of this form of the argument suggests 'monotonicity,' because it is the monotonicity of K with respect to logical implication that justifies the move from (1) to (2).
P-version

1. $K(\alpha \supset \neg H)$ (e.g. (Wryly) You know that if there is a table before you, you aren't a BIAV.)

2. It follows that $K\alpha \supset K\neg H$

3 and 4 are the same as the M-version. The name of the second version has been chosen to suggest 'penetration', since it is by virtue of the 'Penetration Principle'[5]

$$[PP] \ K(\alpha \supset \beta) \supset (K\alpha \supset K\beta)$$

that we move from 1 to 2. Many discussions of this subject take place within the context of *normal* modal logic and, in that context, there is no need to distinguish between the M-version and the P-version.

Having laid all this out, a new strategy will now occur to us. Perhaps we can attack the skeptic not by haggling over premise 3, but rather by questioning the move from 1 to 2. Of course, we must exercise care. If we are to reject the monotonicity or Penetration principles, we must do so in a way which is not simply a thunderbolt of wrath against skepticism.

6.2   General Considerations on Epistemic Logic

As we noted, most epistemic logic, like most philosophical logic in general, is based upon normal modal logic. This

---

[5]This is the terminology of Dretske, (Dretske, 1970)

means that the base logic has a proof-theory given by the rule:

$$[R\Box]\Gamma \vdash \alpha \implies \Box[\Gamma] \vdash \Box\alpha.$$

$$\text{where } \Box[\Gamma] = \{\Box\beta|\beta \in \Gamma\}$$

or alternatively, by the three principles:

$$[RN] \vdash \alpha \implies \vdash \Box\alpha$$
$$[RM] \vdash \alpha \supset \beta \implies \vdash \Box\alpha \supset \Box\beta$$
$$[K] \varnothing \vdash (\Box\alpha \wedge \Box\beta) \supset \Box(\alpha \wedge \beta)$$

It is not that one strives to secure these principles, they obtain on the usual semantics, without effort. In fact, we must struggle to rid ourselves of any of them. Hintikka for example, in his early work at any rate, proves unequal to this struggle and the modal logic upon which his epistemic logic is based, turns out to be normal which leads to the objections we noted earlier.

Decompose deductive closure into its three component principles, and we can see something of which to complain in two of them. The principle [K], of complete aggregation, is the only one not to draw our immediate ire. Though of course if we have [RN] and [RM], [K] will allow the derivation of the Penetration Principle, of recent despised memory.

It has been recorded above that the principle [RN] offends an intuition, quite a central one it might be claimed, according to which all knowledge claims are logically contingent.

As for [RM], we already know where it leads. Both it and [PP] have been subjected to attack in the literature, most notably by Dretske[6]. The burden of these counter-examples is that we are not to be held epistemically responsible for very low-probability 'defeaters.' Suppose those re-

---

[6]In the previously cited (Dretske, 1970).

ally are zebras over there, and that I have a wealth of information about such creatures. I am entitled to say 'I know that those are zebras.' even though a cleverly painted mule could fool me at this distance; indeed even though I *know* that, in these circumstances, a sufficiently unscrupulous and resourceful trickster could make a mule resemble a zebra as near as makes no difference. I don't have to know that they aren't disguised mules, in order to know that they are zebras.

Of course it is open to the skeptic to assert that the Dretske position is simply a (cleverly disguised) argument against the skeptic, and that this is no independent reason to give [RM] and [PP] the go-by. Like many accusations of question-begging, this is double edged. Followers of Dretske are entitled to argue that, on the contrary, making [RM] and [PP] immune to any criticism, is simply begging the question in favor of the skeptic. In any event we shall try to be as accommodating as possible, to the point of making our epistemic logic conform to a skeptical viewpoint, as much as possible. It will turn out to be surprising how far that program can be carried out.

6.3   Constructing a Modal Operator

Normal modal logic can teach us a great deal, even if we are determined to make epistemic logic non-normal. The idea, for example, that a touch-stone of necessity is deductive closure, is one which is part and parcel of the general position now called *preservationism*. This notion has been introduced in an earlier chapter.[7] It makes intuitive sense and also makes certain technical chores go more smoothly than they might otherwise go. For this reason, we choose to generalize from the normal case, rather than simply abandoning it.

---

[7]As well as in the book (Schotch et al., 2009)

The idea here is that our epistemic modality, $K_a \ldots$ ('a knows that...') should also be deductively closed, or alternatively, that it is something that will be preserved by deduction but not classical deduction as that is the hallmark of normal modal logic. Since we are attempting to control the acquisition of [RN] and the rest, we shall define the relation under which K_a *is* closed, indicated by '⊩', by means of:

$$\Gamma \Vdash \alpha \iff \phi[\Gamma] \vdash \phi\alpha$$

Here $\phi[\Gamma]$ is understood as $\{\phi(\beta) | \beta \in \Gamma\}$ as usual.

There are a number of advantages to this formulation. Because we define ⊩ in terms of ⊢ and ϕ in this way, the relation inherits the classical structural rules. Also the modal proof theory will parallel [R□]. Which is to say that, in a sense to be made precise, we have:

$$[\text{RK}] \; \Gamma \Vdash \alpha \implies K_a[\Gamma] \vdash K_a\alpha$$

But does this definition make sense? This is to ask, in the first place, whether it makes sense to call ⊩ an inference relation. The answer would seem to depend in its turn, upon whether or not it makes sense to think of ϕ as a truth operator. If so, then since the definition of ⊩ 'says' that the relation holds whenever the ϕ-truth of the premises guarantees, in the classical sense, the ϕ-truth of the conclusion, it must be some kind of deduction. But when can we say that ϕ is a kind of truth-operator?

This is a question that we have considered in Chapter 5, and we shall be recycling that account here.

In the second place, the definition will make sense in the current context, provided that the notion of inference, whatever other properties it has, gives the rule [RK] some intuitive justification. For example, it should be the kind of inference which bears an interpretation as something like epistemic responsibility. In that case when Γ contains a's

knowledge claims in a certain context, then if $\Gamma \Vdash \alpha$ we are
entitled to hold a epistemically responsible for α in that
context. So in this case at least, it would not be absurd
to hold that a's knowledge is closed with respect to that
notion of inference.

The semantics of K_a is now quite a natural generalization of the normal semantics. Where our semantic struc-
tures contain (non-empty) sets of points (possible worlds)
and an 'accessibility' relation R defined on these, the defi-
nition of truth-at-a-point, indicated by '$\langle \mathcal{M}, u \rangle \vDash$', will contain this clause for K_a:

$$\langle \mathcal{M}, u \rangle \vDash K_a \alpha \iff (\forall v)[Ruv \implies \langle \mathcal{M}, v \rangle \vDash \phi \alpha]$$

Which makes sense if ϕ is recognizably a sort of truth-
operator. Notice also that [RK] is obviously sound (preserves semantic entailment in the class of all semantic struc-
tures) under this condition.

This is also a good way to secure non-normality, since
it will turn out that[8] [RN] and [RM] will preserve validity if
and only if the corresponding ϕ-versions of those rules do,
and that [PP] will be true at every point of every semantic
structure if and only if the ϕ-version of the principle is.

How then should we arrange the semantics of ϕ? We
could realize ϕ as another modal operator with its own
relation—it would have to be a non-normal operator of
course, for K_a to be. This seems a trifle inefficient. If we
had some nice way of giving a relational account of non-
normal modal operators, then why not use that account
for K_a?

Our alternative is to introduce a three-valued logic on
top of which we construct the usual two-valued account of
things. Thus we must use two distinct valuation functions

---

[8]On the above truth-condition for K_a, what we elsewhere called $\vdash^{\phi}$ and $\vdash^{\square}$
are identical.

in our models. All the groundwork for this has been developed in the previously articulated notion of *bisemantic evaluation*,[9] expanded in the usual way to accommodate modality. Previous attempts to combine modal and many-valued semantics have failed to generate anything new[10], but our approach is significantly different from the predecessors.

Part of what motivates us to use (a partially) many-valued semantics is our determination that there be no theorems of the form K_aA. The usual way of removing [RN] in relational semantics is to introduce Q-worlds,[11] worlds at which nothing is necessary. This works well enough as an account of the semantics of logics like **S2**, but leaves behind a restricted version of [RN] according to which all classical tautologies are necessary. On our view, this is as bad as the unrestricted form.

Since K_a will be normal exactly when ϕ is, it soon occurs to us that if the semantics of ϕ involves a logic which has no tautologies, we shall accomplish our end. The easiest way to find such a thing is by using many-valued logic—in particular the so-called strong three-valued tables first developed by Kleene in (Kleene, 1952) 334-335. We first introduced these in chapter 5 but we refresh our memories now:

		β values		
$\alpha \wedge \beta$	T	F	I
α values	T	T	F	I
	F	F	F	F
	I	I	F	I

---

[9]See 110
[10]In this connection see Thomason's important paper (Thomason, 1977).
[11]This is the approach pioneered by Kripke in (Kripke, 1965).

β values

	$\alpha \vee \beta$	T	F	I
	T	T	T	T
α values	F	T	F	I
	I	T	I	I

α	$\neg \alpha$
T	F
F	T
I	I

β values

	$\alpha \supset \beta$	T	F	I
	T	T	F	I
α values	F	T	T	T
	I	T	I	I

6.4 The Logic—A Sketch

Model Theory of Proto-Epistemic Logic

In this section we begin by considering a notion which is a bit wider (or weaker) than knowledge as it is usually understood. Such a notion we shall call *proto*-knowledge, and apply the same modifier to the various technical items of the theory. For example:

Definition 6.4.1. By a (proto-epistemic) *Frame*, we understand a 4-tuple $\mathcal{F} = \langle \mathbb{U}, \mathbb{L}, \mathbb{C}, \mathbb{R} \rangle$, where $\mathbb{U}$ is a non-empty set (the set of points), $(\mathbb{L}, \mathbb{C})$ is a partition of $\mathbb{U}$, and $\mathbb{R}$ is a binary relation defined over $\mathbb{U}$.

Definition 6.4.2. By a (proto-epistemic) Model, we understand a pair $\mathcal{M} = \langle \mathcal{F}, E \rangle$, where $\mathcal{F}$ is a

proto-epistemic frame, and E is a bisemantic evaluation defined as follows:
$E = \langle V, \Phi \rangle$ where

> V, the *primary* truth-value assignment, is a function from **At** $\times$ $\mathbb{U}$ into $\{1, 0\}$

> Φ, the *secondary* truth-value assignment, is a function from **At** $\times$ $\mathbb{U}$ into $\{T, F, I\}$,

> here **At** is the set of atomic formulas.

Relative to a proto-epistemic model $\mathcal{M}$, we recursively define two notions of truth at the point u. The first, less familiar one, is called the *secondary* value of a formula α, at a point $u \in \mathbb{U}$, relative to the bi-semantic evaluation of the proto-epistemic model $\mathcal{M}$, represented by the notation: $\|\alpha, u\|_{\mathcal{M}}$ defined:

Definition 6.4.3. $\|\alpha, u\|_{\mathcal{M}}$, is defined inductively:

If $\alpha \in$ **At** then $\|\alpha, u\|_{\mathcal{M}} = \Phi(\alpha)$, where Φ is the secondary truth-value assignment of E.

If α is a classical compound, then $\|\alpha, u\|_{\mathcal{M}}$ is computed via the strong tables.

If $\alpha = \phi\beta$ then $\|\alpha, u\|_{\mathcal{M}} = \|\beta, u\|_{\mathcal{M}}$. This is referred to as the *transparency* condition.

If $\alpha = K_a\beta$ then $\|\alpha, u\|_{\mathcal{M}} = I$

Next we have the more familiar general concept of truth at a point u, of a proto-epistemic model $\mathcal{M}$, indicated by $\langle \mathcal{M}, u \rangle \vDash$.

The basis clause for atomic formulas is the usual one using the primary truth-value assignment, although we have two new atomic sentences (but only in the primary language) $\mathbb{L}$ and $\mathbb{C}$ which have the expected clauses:

[$\mathbb{L}$] $\langle \mathcal{M}, u \rangle \vDash \mathbb{L} \iff u \in \mathbb{L}$

[$\mathbb{C}$] $\langle \mathcal{M}, u \rangle \vDash \mathbb{C} \iff u \in \mathbb{C}$

The recursion clauses for the classical compounds go as usual. For the rest, we have:

[KN] $\langle \mathcal{M}, u \rangle \vDash K_a \alpha \iff (\forall v)(\mathbb{R}uv \implies \langle \mathcal{M}, v \rangle \vDash \phi\alpha)$

[$\phi 1$] If $u \in \mathbb{L}, \langle \mathcal{M}, u \rangle \vDash \phi\alpha \iff \|\alpha, u\|_{\mathcal{M}} = T$ or I

[$\phi 2$] If $u \in \mathbb{C}, \langle \mathcal{M}, u \rangle \vDash \phi P \iff \|P, u\|_{\mathcal{M}} = T$

It will be useful in the statement of proof principles to have in hand some notation for the dual of our truth-operator ϕ.

Definition 6.4.4.

$$\psi(\alpha) \text{ for } \neg\phi\neg(\alpha)$$

Part of what it means to say that ϕ is a truth-operator, is that ψ is also a truth operator.

Given the clauses for ϕ, it is easy to see that the derived clauses for [$\psi 1$] and [$\psi 2$] are the same as [$\phi 2$] and [$\phi 1$] respectively (with ψ for ϕ).

Some Notes on the Semantics

From an earlier discussion (see page 62) of this kind of approach to modal logic, We know that if ϕ has any of the properties which correspond to [RN], [RM] or [K], then its associated notion of necessity will have them too. The operator ϕ just introduced has neither of the first two of those properties, which means we cannot prove (by the earlier argument) that K_a has either of them. But we require more here—a proof that they don't hold rather than the lack of a proof that they do.

If we knew that the relation defined by

Definition 6.4.5. '$\Gamma \vdash^{K_a} P$' for '$K_a[\Gamma] \vdash K_a(P)$'

---

is the same relation (in the extensional sense) as the relation $\vdash^\phi$, introduced earlier, this would establish the result straight away, but we aren't yet in a position to obtain this.

However, we can certainly establish immediately that neither [RN] nor [RM] preserve semantic entailment in the class of proto-epistemic models and that the principle [PP] is not logically true, ditto.

The key is our division of the points into $\mathbb{L}$(iberal) and $\mathbb{C}$(onservative) camps. Since the value I persists, (which is to say that if all the atoms of any formula take the value I, so does the formula) there are no formulas (in the language of classical logic) which take the value T on every Φ, i.e. no 3-valued tautologies (in the language of classical logic[12]. For α any classical tautology, since $\phi\alpha$ is only true at any $\mathbb{C}$-point u, if $\|\alpha, u\|_{\mathcal{M}} = T$, under any evaluation which drives the secondary value of α to I, $\phi\alpha$ must fail at u in $\mathcal{M}$. We can then construct a new model $\mathcal{M}'$ which differs from $\mathcal{M}$ only in that $\mathbb{U}' = \mathbb{U} \cup \{*\}$ where $*$ is a point not in $\mathbb{U}$, and $\langle *, u \rangle \in \mathbb{R}'$. It is easy to see that $K_a(\alpha)$ must fail at $*$ in $\mathcal{M}'$ since $\phi\alpha$ fails at u.

To find a counterexample to [RM], we need only evaluate a classical tautology like $\alpha \supset (\beta \vee \neg\beta)$ at point $u \in \mathbb{C}$ where

---

[12]this assumes, of course, that $\bot$ (with the obvious semantics) is not part of the language

$\|\alpha, u\|_{\mathcal{M}} = T$ and $\|\beta, u\|_{\mathcal{M}} = I$, or a formula $(\alpha \wedge \neg \alpha) \supset \beta$ at point $v \in \mathbb{L}$ such that $\|\alpha, v\|_{\mathcal{M}} = I$ and $\|\beta, v\|_{\mathcal{M}} = F$. In either case, ϕ(antecedent) does not imply ϕ(consequent) and another 'lead in' argument establishes that K_a(antecedent) does not imply K_a(consequent).

The fate of [PP] is sealed at a point $v \in \mathbb{L}$ for which $\|\alpha, v\|_{\mathcal{M}} = I$ and $\|\beta, v\|_{\mathcal{M}} = F$. At such a point, $\|\alpha \supset \beta, v\|_{\mathcal{M}} = I$, so $\langle \mathcal{M}, v \rangle \vDash \phi(\alpha \supset \beta)$, $\langle \mathcal{M}, v \rangle \vDash \phi\alpha$ but $\langle \mathcal{M}, v \rangle \nvDash \phi\beta$.

Interpretation Issues

We know already that the operator ϕ (and it's dual ψ) has the strong distribution properties (over $\wedge$ and $\vee$ respectively) that we require for truth operators. This provides a measure of confidence in our definition of $\Vdash$ but opens the question of informal interpretation.

Given the epistemic setting, it might be suggested that ϕ be interpreted informally along the lines of 'It is reasonable to accept that ...' The idea is that the values T, F, I are assigned on the basis of some test or measurement. Under such an interpretation, the value I would mean that the test misfires somehow, or that there is no test for the sentence in question.

As matters now stand, we cannot plausibly interpret '$K_a(\alpha)$' as 'a knows that α,' because the truth of α, or even it's ϕ-truth need not follow from $K_a(\alpha)$. For the latter, we need only impose the relational condition of reflexivity:

$$(\forall u)\mathbb{R}uu$$

on every proto-epistemic frame. Once that condition holds, it is easy to see the $\phi\alpha$ now follows from $K_a(\alpha)$ which, under our interpretation, is to say that $K_a(P)$ implies that it is reasonable to accept that P.

This cannot be done blithely however. Our previous 'lead-in' argument, which provided a counterexample to the K_a version of [RM] is vulnerable as soon as we make any changes to $\mathbb{R}$. We had discovered a tautology of the form $\alpha \supset \beta$ such that there is a model $\mathcal{M}$ which may assume without loss of generality, contains a point $v \in \mathbb{C}$ such that $\|\alpha, v\|_{\mathcal{M}} = T$ and $\|\beta, v\|_{\mathcal{M}} = I$. Thus, at v, $\langle \mathcal{M}, v \rangle \vDash \phi\alpha$ and $\langle \mathcal{M}, v \rangle \nvDash \phi\beta$. We then constructed a new model $\mathcal{M}'$ such that $\mathbb{U}' = \mathbb{U} \cup \{u\}$ where $u \notin \mathbb{U}$ and $\mathbb{R}' = \mathbb{R} \cup \{\langle u, v \rangle\}$. The evaluation E' agrees with E and the fate of u is a don't care as far as V and Φ are concerned. However the atomic formulas are evaluated at u, it must be the case that $\langle \mathcal{M}, u \rangle \vDash K_a(\alpha)$ and $\langle \mathcal{M}, u \rangle \nvDash K_a(\beta)$.

If $\mathbb{R}$ is suddenly made reflexive, this has no effect on the latter, but we no longer have assurance that $\langle \mathcal{M}, u \rangle \vDash K_a(\alpha)$ still holds. This is because in the new model we must now have that $\mathbb{R}' = \mathbb{R} \cup \{\langle u, u \rangle, \langle u, v \rangle\}$. The fate of u under E' is no longer a don't care, since we can only employ an E' on which $\langle \mathcal{M}, u \rangle \vDash \phi\alpha$. We know that such a thing is possible because $\langle \mathcal{M}, v \rangle \vDash \phi\alpha$.

So, to resolve all our worries, we need a stipulation to the effect that the behavior of u with respect to E', exactly matches the behavior of v with respect to E, at least as far as all of the atomic subformulas of α. Everything else remains a don't care.[13]

Having gained reassurance that we haven't inadvertently acquired the monotonicity of K_a, we need to ask some hard questions.

(1) What is the intuitive basis of the frame relation $\mathbb{R}$?

(2) What is the connection, if any, between K_a and the usual account of 'a knows that ...?'

---

[13] Somebody might wonder why we don't save ourselves the trouble of leading in a new point when we now *have* a point, namely v which is related to v. The answer is that we don't know which other points v is related to. But when we lead in u in the new model, we stipulate that it is related exactly to itself and v.

Such questions are obviously interrelated. To begin with, we shall propose that, since the secondary truth-values are supposed to record the result of a test or measurement, the most plausible role for $\mathbb{R}$ would be to pick out at each point u, the set of points v which are relevant to performing tests or measurements at u. Putting these informal moves together we now want an interpretation of $\langle \mathcal{M}, u \rangle \vDash K_a(\alpha)$. In terms of the newly minted motivation, we would read the expression on the right along the lines of: 'α has passed the appropriate test (or: it is reasonable to accept that α) in every relevant testing context (including we would now say, the current context).'

Is that enough to interpret K_a as knowledge? Lots of epistemologists would presumably say 'No!'—would say that knowledge must in addition imply truth. We can agree with this proviso, but we need a model-theoretic condition to secure the property rather than a condition on frames (as would be the case for simple alethic necessity). In other words we must change the truth-condition as follows:

Definition 6.4.6. We obtain the definition of truth at a point for *epistemic* (as opposed to proto-epistemic) logic, if we augment the [K]-clause with:

$$\text{and } \langle \mathcal{M}, u \rangle \vDash \alpha.$$

Our agreement to this revision is conditional upon not losing the proof that [RM] fails to preserve semantic entailment in the class of epistemic models. A moment's thought should suffice to reassure us that since the antecedent α of the tautology $\alpha \supset \beta$ might be an atomic formula, there is no problem in making sure that $\langle \mathcal{M}, u \rangle \vDash \alpha$ at the lead-in point u.

Is *this* now sufficient? Do we have real knowledge at

last? The matter isn't entirely clear even though there are certainly suggestive echoes. Not surprisingly, we would suggest that our notion of K_a is close to what Dretske meant by knowledge in (Dretske, 1970). Consider the zebra/mule case again.

Even though you are a world-authority on zebras, the skeptic will insist that you do not *know* that those animals in the middle distance are in fact zebras, since a tricked-out mule could fool you at this distance. What's at issue is that the proposition α = 'Those creatures over there are zebras.' hasn't passed every test. In particular, α hasn't passed the test of checking to see if the apparent zebras are actually mules. Of course this is only the thin edge of the wedge. Once you agree to perform that test before registering a knowledge claim, there will be demands for yet other tests, until at length you acknowledge that there are tests that you cannot perform.[14] This is what would happen if you agree to 'every test (no matter how absurd)' rather than 'every relevant test.' Once we realize that, we can see the necessity for digging in our heels.

And it isn't hard to see that requiring only relevant tests be passed, amounts to an endorsement of the current truth-condition. Notice also that [PP] fails on this semantics. For if the mule-test isn't relevant, then even though it follows as a matter of logic that $\alpha \supset \beta$ (where β = 'Those aren't mules.'), it isn't true that $K_{you}\alpha \supset K_{you}\beta$, since although the relevant tests for α have been passed, at least one of the tests for β has not been passed since it wasn't relevant.

But what has happened to the role of belief in all this? Isn't it usual to require that if a knows that α, then a must believe that α? Actually the usual requirement is a bit stronger, amounting to a must have a *justified* belief that α.

---

[14]How, for instance, would you test to see if you are actually a brain in a vat?

Justified belief would seem to be compatible with the truth condition we have just obtained. To say that a does not believe that α, or that a's belief is not justified, is surely to say that α has failed a(t least one) relevant test. We might want to interpret the truth of $\phi\alpha$ at u, required by the reflexivity of $\mathbb{R}$ to amount to a's belief. The whole set of successes in all relevant contexts might be further interpreted as a justification for a's belief. Notice that this account makes justification depend upon the context of evaluation. α might be justified in one context (model, point) but not at another. Such variance would seem to be an obvious feature of any adequate notion of justification.

But now we must deal with a difficulty first raised by Russell[15]. Knowledge cannot be identified with justified true belief in those cases in which the belief is derived from a falsehood. Russell's example is:

> If a man believes that the late Prime Minister's last name began with a B he believes what is true since the late Prime Minister was Sir Henry Campbell Bannerman. But if he believes that Mr. Balfour was the late Prime Minister, he will still believe that the late Prime Minister's last name began with a B, yet this belief though true, would not be thought to constitute knowledge.

The belief may be true and justified, but the justification may depend upon a falsehood. In Russell's case the belief that the last name began with B is justified by the belief that the person in question was Sir Henry which, we must assume, is justified. A later (though perhaps no better) example, due to Gettier,[16] uses disjunctive beliefs. I may have a true belief in $\alpha \vee \beta$ because I believe (with justification) that α, whereas it is β which is the only true disjunct.

[15](Russell, 1912) 131-132
[16]in his (Gettier, 1963)

We should notice that Gettier's example depends crucially upon the monotonicity of 'a is justified in believing that α.' which is by no means beyond the bounds of controversy. In particular, if we were to analyze a is justified in believing that α at u, as $\phi\alpha$ is true in all testing contexts v, which are relevant to u, as we might, then our account is immune to Gettier's problem (at least the way that he stated it) and perhaps also to Russell's since the monotonicity of justification fails.

According to Lehrer, in (Lehrer, 1974), there have been a number of defences against Russell/Gettier counterexamples which reject monotonicity for justification.[17] Lehrer himself, in the work just cited, proposes an account of justification which turns out to be non-monotonic. Nevertheless, we are inclined to think that the account we give is the first one to present a formalized account of non-monotonicity for justification, and hence for knowledge.

Skeptical Issues

One of the features of this approach to epistemic logic, is how very skeptical it is. Under our intuitive interpretation of ϕ as an operator which records the result of a test of some kind, it turns out that sentences of the form $K_a\alpha$ never test out true (T). At best, a knowledge claim might be acceptable at an $\mathbb{L}$-point, but never at a $\mathbb{C}$-point.

All those contexts in which a knowledge claim is acceptable are ones in which the negation of that claim is also acceptable and in any context in which the negation of a knowledge claim is not acceptable, neither is the claim. To put the matter formally:

$$\phi(K_a\alpha) \equiv \phi(\neg K_a\alpha)$$

---

[17]Lehrer mentions in particular Thalberg, Margolis and Pailthorp as advocating a non-monotonic account of justification. See Lehrer (1974) p. 216

is logically true in the class of epistemic models.

And since this is independent of the formula α, it would seem to be no more than a way of saying that all knowledge claims have a very dubious status. Not to put too fine a point on it, what more would be needed, to call this analysis 'skeptical?'

A hot-blooded skeptic might urge that it isn't enough for knowledge claims to be acceptable only when their negations are. Real, full-contact skepticism requires that knowledge claims one and all be *false*. Alas this is a bit too strong to be coherent. For consider: if $K_a\alpha$ takes F at every point then $\neg K_a\alpha$ is going to have to take T. That means that $\phi(\neg K_a\alpha)$ will be logically true in the class of epistemic models, which in turn guarantees the logical truth of $K_a\neg K_a\alpha$.

So the hard-line version of skepticism has as a consequence that there are logical truths of the form $K_a\alpha$, which isn't very skeptical at all, as well as offending one of our cherished principles concerning the contingency of knowledge.

But if this semantics really is skeptical in any useful sense it would seem to provide some basis for an impression that many people have, which is that skepticism has a lot of internal tension, to put the matter as gently as possible. In this formal approach we seem to have shown that the tenets of the skeptic are compatible with the failure of the skeptical argument. A puzzle if not a paradox.

Epistemic Logic and 'Modal Reduction'

In normal modal logic, we study the logical relations between strings of iterated modal operators (modal reduction theory, so-called) as part of frame theory. By restricting the class of models to those in which the frame relation satisfies this or that condition, we obtain logics with this or that reduction theory.

For example, to obtain a (normal) logic in which the famous (or infamous):

$$[KK] \; K_a P \supset K_a K_a P$$

holds, one restricts the class of models to those in which the frame relation is transitive.

The current approach to the model theory of epistemic logic has very little utility in questions concerning reduction theory. To say that e.g. $K_a K_a \alpha$ is false at a point u of a model $\mathcal{M}$ is *not* to say that $K_a \alpha$ is false at some related point v, but rather to say that $\phi(K_a \alpha)$ is false there. Now even if u is related to whatever points v is, nothing much follows (so far) about the fate of $K_a \alpha$ at u. So we no longer have a demonstration that [KK] is logically true in the class of transitive models.

But even if transitivity of $\mathbb{R}$ *did* imply some interesting reduction principle, we would be loath to adopt that restriction. We think of epistemic logic as requiring the failure of the principle of monotonicity for K_a, such failure answering to our intuitions concerning epistemic responsibility and perhaps also to certain worries about the counter-examples of Russell and Gettier.

In order to assure ourselves that [RM] doesn't preserve semantic entailment in the class of epistemic models, we had to resort to a so-called lead-in argument in which we construct a new model given an existing model which contains a point of a certain kind. We know this sort of argument will work in the class of epistemic models, because we know that if $\mathbb{R}uv$ then even if $\mathbb{R}vx$ for many other points x, we don't need to worry about u being accidentally related to any of them. Once transitivity rears its ugly head, we have those worries. There is no guarantee that epistemic logic will remain non-monotonic, once $\mathbb{R}$ is transitive.

Proof Theory of Epistemic Logic

We organize the proof-theory of epistemic logic into a number of categories which together characterize a logic which we call *EL*.

Definitions

> '$\psi\alpha$' for '$\neg\phi\neg\alpha$'
>
> '$\delta[\Gamma]$' for '$\{\delta\alpha \mid \alpha \in \Gamma\}$'
>
> '$\Gamma \Vdash \alpha$' for '$\phi[\Gamma] \vdash \phi\alpha$'

'Truth' Principles

We take over these from our previous discussion of bi-semantics. See page 114

> $$\phi(\alpha \wedge \beta) \longleftrightarrow \phi\alpha \wedge \phi\beta$$
> $$\phi(\alpha \vee \beta) \longleftrightarrow \phi\alpha \vee \phi\beta$$
> $$\psi(\alpha \wedge \beta) \longleftrightarrow \psi\alpha \wedge \psi\beta$$
> $$\psi(\alpha \vee \beta) \longleftrightarrow \psi\alpha \vee \psi\beta$$
> $$\vdash \alpha \equiv \beta \implies \vdash \phi\alpha \equiv \phi\beta$$
> $$\vdash \alpha \equiv \beta \implies \vdash \psi\alpha \equiv \psi\beta$$

In the following ∂ is any finite string consisting of zero or more occurrences of ϕ, and ψ, and zero or an even number of occurrences of $\neg$.

> $$\psi\alpha \longleftrightarrow \psi\partial\alpha$$
> $$\phi\alpha \longleftrightarrow \phi\partial\alpha$$
> $$\psi\neg\alpha \longleftrightarrow \psi\neg\partial\alpha$$
> $$\phi\neg\alpha \longleftrightarrow \phi\neg\partial\alpha$$

'Political' Principles

> $$\mathbb{L} \underline{\vee} \mathbb{C}$$

$$\mathbb{L} \supset \neg(\psi\alpha \wedge \psi\neg\alpha)$$
$$\mathbb{C} \supset \neg(\phi\alpha \wedge \phi\neg\alpha)$$

'Equivalence' Principles

$$\partial(\neg(\alpha \supset \beta)) \longleftrightarrow \partial(\alpha \wedge \neg\beta)$$
$$\partial(\alpha) \longleftrightarrow \partial(\neg\neg\alpha)$$

Modal Principles

$[K_a]\ \Gamma \Vdash \alpha \implies K_a[\Gamma] \vdash K_a\alpha$

$[\mathbb{L}K_a]\ \mathbb{L} \supset (\phi K_a\alpha \wedge \phi\neg K_a\alpha)$

$[\mathbb{C}K_a]\ \mathbb{C} \supset (\neg\phi K_a\alpha \wedge (\neg\phi\neg K_a\alpha)$

$[K_aT]\ K_a\alpha \supset \alpha$

$[K_aT\phi]\ K_a\alpha \supset \phi\alpha$

6.5 Metalogic of Epistemic Logic

Definition 6.5.1. $\mathcal{M}_{EL}$, *the EL-canonical model,* is defined to be the tuple:
$(\mathbb{U}_{EL}, \mathbb{L}_{EL}, \mathbb{C}_{EL}, \mathbb{R}_{EL}, V_{EL}, \Phi_{EL})$ where:

$\mathbb{U}_{EL}$ is the set of maximally *EL*-consistent sets of formulas

$\Delta \in \mathbb{L}_{EL} \iff [\Delta \in \mathbb{U}_{EL} \text{ and } \Delta \vdash \mathbb{L}]$

$\Delta \in \mathbb{C}_{EL} \iff [\Delta \in \mathbb{U}_{EL} \text{ and } \Delta \vdash \mathbb{C}]$

For all $\Sigma, \Delta \in \mathbb{U}_{EL} : \mathbb{R}_{EL}\Sigma\Delta \iff (\forall\alpha)(\Sigma \vdash K_a\alpha \implies \Delta \vdash \phi\alpha)$

For all $\alpha \in \mathbf{At}$ and
$\Sigma \in \mathbb{U}_{EL} : V_{EL}(\alpha, \Sigma) = 1 \iff \Sigma \vdash \alpha$

For all $\alpha \in$ **At** and
$\Sigma \in \mathbb{L}_{EL} : \Phi_{EL}(\alpha, \Sigma) = T \iff \Sigma \vdash \psi\alpha$,

$\Phi_{EL}(\alpha, \Sigma) = F \iff \Sigma \vdash \psi(\neg\alpha)$,

$\Phi_{EL}(\alpha, \Sigma) = I \iff \Sigma \vdash \phi(\alpha) \land \phi(\neg\alpha)$

For all $\alpha \in$ **At** and
$\Sigma \in \mathbb{C}_{EL} : \Phi_{EL}(\alpha, \Sigma) = T \iff \Sigma \vdash \phi\alpha$,

$\Phi_{EL}(\alpha, \Sigma) = F \iff \Sigma \vdash \phi(\neg\alpha)$,

$\Phi_{EL}(\alpha, \Sigma) = I \iff \Sigma \vdash \psi(\alpha) \land \psi(\neg\alpha)$

Lemma 6.5.2 (Φ_{EL} Lemma). *For all formulas α*

($\mathbb{L}_{EL}$) *For all $\Sigma \in \mathbb{L}_{EL}$:*

$\|\alpha, \Sigma\|_{\mathcal{M}_{EL}} = T \iff \Sigma \vdash \psi\alpha$

$\|\alpha, \Sigma\|_{\mathcal{M}_{EL}} = F \iff \Sigma \vdash \psi\neg\alpha$

$\|\alpha, \Sigma\|_{\mathcal{M}_{EL}} = I \iff \Sigma \vdash \phi\alpha \land \phi(\neg\alpha)$

($\mathbb{C}_{EL}$) *For all $\Sigma \in \mathbb{C}_{EL}$:*

$\|\alpha, \Sigma\|_{\mathcal{M}_{EL}} = T \iff \Sigma \vdash \phi\alpha$

$\|\alpha, \Sigma\|_{\mathcal{M}_{EL}} = F \iff \Sigma \vdash \phi\neg\alpha$

$\|\alpha, \Sigma\|_{\mathcal{M}_{EL}} = I \iff \Sigma \vdash \psi\alpha \land \psi(\neg\alpha)$

Proof. The proof is by a routine induction on the structure of α, with the basis step handled by the definition of Φ_{EL}. In the induction step, the non-modal cases are handled exactly as in the proof of the corresponding result for non-modal bi-semantics (see page ??). For the modal cases we show only the case where α is of the form $K_a\beta$, and $\Sigma \in \mathbb{L}_{EL}$.

$\|K_a\beta, \Sigma\|_{\mathcal{M}_{EL}} \neq T$ or F by the secondary truth-condition

$\|K_a\beta, \Sigma\|_{\mathcal{M}_{EL}} = I \iff \|\beta, \Sigma, \mathcal{M}_{EL}\| = T$ or F or I, by the truth-condition. Of course the right-hand side of this is always true. By [$\mathbb{L}K_a$] so is: $\mathbb{L} \supset (\phi K_a\alpha \wedge \phi\neg K_a\alpha)$, and since $\Sigma \in \mathbb{L}_{EL} \iff \Sigma \vdash \mathbb{L}$, it follows that $\|K_a\alpha, \Sigma\|_{\mathcal{M}_{EL}} = I \iff \Sigma \vdash (\phi K_a\alpha \wedge \phi\neg K_a\alpha)$.

$\square$

Next, we require the epistemic version of a standard result from the metalogic of normal modal logic the R_L^+ Lemma on page 50.

Lemma 6.5.3 ($\mathbb{R}_{EL}$ Lemma). *For all formulas α, and all $\Sigma \in \mathbb{U}_{EL}$:*
$\Sigma \vdash K_a\alpha \iff$ *for all $\Delta \in \mathbb{U}_{EL}$: $\mathbb{R}_{EL}\Sigma, \Delta \implies \Delta \vdash \phi\alpha$*

Proof. The only-if direction ($\implies$) follows immediately from the definition of $\mathbb{R}_{EL}$. For the converse we argue indirectly.

Assume that $\Sigma \nvdash K_a\alpha$.

We shall prove the existence of some $\Delta \in \mathbb{U}_{EL}$ such that $\mathbb{R}_{EL}\Sigma, \Delta$ and $\Delta \nvdash \phi\alpha$.

Evidently every Δ to which Σ is related by $\mathbb{R}_{EL}$ must contain the set $core(\Sigma) = \phi[K_a(\Sigma)]$.

So in order to demonstrate the existence of the required Δ, it suffices to show that $core(\Sigma) \cup \{\neg\phi\alpha\} \nvdash \perp$.

> Suppose to the contrary that the set is inconsistent,
> then $core(\Sigma) \vdash \phi\alpha$ by [$\neg$E].
> In other words, $K_a(\Sigma) \Vdash \alpha$.
> It follows that $K_a[K_a(\Sigma)] \vdash K_a\alpha$ by the rule [K_a].
> But $K_a[K_a(\Sigma)] \subseteq \Sigma$.
> So $\Sigma \vdash K_a\alpha$, contrary to hypothesis.

Thus $core(\Sigma) \cup \{\neg\phi\alpha\}$ must be consistent after all, and that set can be expanded in the standard way to the required Δ.

So, by contraposition,
for all $\Delta \in \mathbb{U}_{EL}(\mathbb{R}_{EL}\Sigma, \Delta \implies \Delta \vdash \phi\alpha) \implies \Sigma \vdash K_a\alpha$

$\square$

With these results we can easily derive the theorem, sometimes called the *fundamental theorem* (for *EL*) which records a crucial property of the canonical model.

Theorem 6.5.4. *For every formula α and $\Sigma \in \mathbb{U}_{EL}$:*
$\langle \mathcal{M}_{EL}, \Sigma \rangle \vDash \alpha \iff \Sigma \vdash \alpha.$

Proof. The proof is by induction on the length of the formula α. In the basis case when $\alpha \in$ **At** or $\alpha = \mathbb{L}$ or $\mathbb{C}$, the result is trivial by the definitions of V_{EL}, $\mathbb{L}_{EL}$, and $\mathbb{C}_{EL}$ respectively.

In the induction step, the classical non-modal cases are handled in the usual way. We consider only the cases $[\phi]$ $\alpha = \phi\beta$ and $[K_a]$ $\alpha = K_a\beta$.

$[\phi]$ We wish to show that $\langle \mathcal{M}_{EL}, \Sigma \rangle \vDash \phi\beta \iff \Sigma \vdash \phi\beta$.

First assume that $\Sigma \in \mathbb{L}_{EL}$. Then $\langle \mathcal{M}_{EL}, \Sigma \rangle \vDash \phi\beta$
$\iff \|\beta, \Sigma\|_{\mathcal{M}_{EL}} = T$ or I, and by the previous lemma (Φ_{EL} lemma)
$\iff \Sigma \vdash \phi\beta \wedge \phi\neg\beta$ or $\Sigma \vdash \psi\beta$. Both disjuncts imply $\Sigma \vdash \phi\beta$ but the latter also implies one or the other of the disjuncts by maximality of Σ. QED

Finally, assume that $\Sigma \in \mathbb{C}_{EL}$. Then $\langle \mathcal{M}_{EL}, \Sigma \rangle \vDash \phi\beta$
$\iff \|\beta, \Sigma\|_{\mathcal{M}_{EL}} = T$ and by the previous lemma
$\iff \Sigma \vdash \phi\beta$. QED

$[K_a]$ We wish to show that
$\langle \mathcal{M}_{EL}, \Sigma \rangle \vDash K_a\beta \iff \Sigma \vdash K_a\beta.$

$\langle \mathcal{M}_{EL}, \Sigma \rangle \vDash K_a \beta$
$\iff$ for every $\Delta \in \mathbb{U}_{EL} : \mathbb{R}_{EL}\Sigma, \Delta \implies \langle \mathcal{M}_{EL}, \Delta \rangle \vDash \phi\beta$
by the truth-condition. By the previous case
$\iff$ for every $\Delta \in \mathbb{U}_{EL} : \mathbb{R}_{EL}\Sigma, \Delta \implies \Delta \vdash \phi\beta$ and by
the $\mathbb{R}_{EL}$ lemma
$\iff \Sigma \vdash K_a\beta$.

$\square$

And these results lead to the *EL* version of an equivalence theorem.

Theorem 6.5.5 (Equivalence Theorem for *EL*). *The following are equivalent:*

(1) $\Gamma \vdash \alpha$

(2) $\Gamma \vDash \alpha$

(3) For all epistemic models $\mathcal{M}$: $\vDash^{\mathcal{M}} \Gamma \implies \vDash^{\mathcal{M}} \alpha$

(4) $\vDash^{\mathcal{M}_{EL}} \Gamma \implies \vDash^{\mathcal{M}_{EL}} \alpha$

Proof. (1) $\implies$ (2) by the usual 'soundness' argument, while (2) $\implies$ (3) since (3) is the definition of (2). (3) $\implies$ (4) since $\mathcal{M}_{EL}$ is an epistemic model. Finally, suppose that (1) is false, i.e. $\Gamma \nvdash \alpha$. It follows by a familiar argument that $\Gamma \cup \{\neg\alpha\}$ is *EL*-consistent, and hence there must be some $\Delta \in \mathbb{U}_{EL}$ of which Γ is a subset and which doesn't prove α (since it proves $\neg\alpha$). Thus in the canonical model Γ is true at Δ and α isn't. Thus (4) is false. Thus by contraposition, (4) $\implies$ (1). $\square$

Evidently we could also prove that (3) $\implies$ (2) and that (1) $\implies$ (4). We leave open the question of whether (3) $\implies$ (2).

With the aid of the equivalence theorem we can answer questions that were raised at the start of our epistemic enterprize. Since entailment and provability are equivalent in epistemic logic, we know that, since (the epistemic equivalents of) neither [RM] nor [RN] preserve entailment in the class of epistemic models neither of the rules is derivable in epistemic logic. We also know, just from $(1) \implies (2)$, that [PP] is not logically true in the class of epistemic models. Finally, we know that the relation defined:

$$\Gamma \vdash^{K_a} \alpha \iff K_a[\Gamma] \vdash K_a\alpha$$

is the same relation as $\Vdash$.

Index of Symbols

$\mathbb{M}_L$ class of L-maximally consistent sets, page 49

$\Diamond$ possibility connective, page 35

$\vdash_{\text{Ł}3}$ proves in Ł3, page 84

⌖, £   context indicating sentential constants, page 110

$\mathbb{M}(\Sigma, R)$ the maximal prime extension of Σ relative to y, page 98

max(Δ) Δ is maximal, page 22

$\mathbb{M}_{\text{Ł}3}(\Sigma)$ Σ is an Ł3 maximally consistent set, page 87

$\models \alpha$ α is logically true, page 13

$\neg$ object language negation, page 4

$\|P\|_E$ secondary truth-value relative to the bi-semantic evaluation E, page 111

$\|\alpha, u\|_{\mathcal{M}}$ secondary truth-value relative to the bi-semantic evaluation E at a point u of a proto-epistemic model $\mathcal{M}$, page 139

$\|\alpha\|_{ij}$ (3-valued)truth-value of the formula α relative to a truth-value assignment $v - ij$, page 76

$\overline{\alpha}$ α is not true in Ł3, page 83

$\perp$ *falsum* symbol, page 4

ϕ truth operator, page 58

$\phi(\alpha)$ α is ϕ-true, page 135

£ $\neg$⌖, page 111

$\vdash^{K_a}$ epistemic inference relation, page 141

$\vdash^{\phi}$ ϕ-inference, page 60

[RN]   rule of normality (unrestricted necessitation), page 42

[R]   Rule of Reflexivity, page 8

[T*]   Alternative Rule of Transitivity, page 9

[T]   Rule of Transitivity (Cut), page 9

[W]   Wittgenstein's Law (of atomicity), page 9

COMP completeness predicate, page 15

CONJ Conjunctive predicate, page 15

IMPLIC implicativity predicate, page 15

PRIME Primeness predicate, page 15

THEORY(Δ) Δ is a theory, page 14

TH3(Δ) Δ is an Ł3 theory, page 84

Ł3   3-valued logic based on the Ł3 $\supset$, page 75

Index

References

Becker, O. (1930). Zur logick der modalitäten. *Jahrbuch für Philosophie und Phönomenologische Forschung*, 497–548.

Churchman, C. W. (1942). Towards a general logic of propositions. In *Philosophical Essays in Honor of Edgar Arthur Singer Jr.*, pp. 46–68. University of Pennsylvania Press.

Cresswell, M. J. and G. E. Hughes (1968). *An Introduction to Modal Logic.* Methuen.

Dretske, F. (1970). Epistemic operators. *Journal of Philosophy*, 1–22.

Fine, K. (1975). Some connections between elementary and modal logic. In *Proceedings of the Third Scandinavian Logic Symposium (Univ. Uppsala, Uppsala, 1973)*, Amsterdam, pp. 15–51. Stud. Logic Found. Math., Vol. 82. North-Holland.

Gettier, E. J. (1963). Is justified true belief knowledge? *Analysis xxiii*, 121–3.

Gődel (1933). Eine interpretation des intuitionistischer aussagenkalküls. *Ergebnisse eines mathematisches Kolloquiums 4*, 34–40.

Hacking, I. (1979). What is logic. *Journal of Philosophy 76*(6), 285–319.

Hintikka (1962). *Knowledge and Belief.* Ithica: Cornell University Press.

Kleene, S. C. (1952). *Introduction to Metamathematics*. Van Nostrand.

Kripke, S. A. (1963). Semantic analysis of modal logic i, normal propositional calculi. *Zeitschrift für mathematische logik und Grundlagen der Mathematik 9*, 67–96.

Kripke, S. A. (1965). Semantical analysis of modal logic ii, non-normal modal propositional calculi. In J. W. Addison, L. Henkin, and A. Tarski (Eds.), *The THeory of Models*, pp. 206–220. Amsterdam: North Holland Publishing Co.

Lapierre, S. and F. Lepage (1999). Completeness and representation theorem for epistemic states in first-order predicate calculus. *Logica Trianguli 3*, 85–109.

Lehrer, K. (1974). *Knowledge*. Oxford.

Lemmon, E. (1957). New foundations for lewis modal systems. *The Journal of Symbolic Logic 22*, 176–186.

Lewis, C. (1918a). *A survey of symbolic logic*. Berkeley: University of California Press. Semicentennial Publications of the University of California.

Lewis, C. I. (1913). Interresting theorems in symbolic logic. *Journal of Philosophy 10*, 239–242.

Lewis, C. I. (1914a). The matrix algebra for implication. *Journal of Philosophy 11*, 589–600.

Lewis, C. I. (1914b). A new algebra of strict implication. *Mind 23*, 240–247.

Lewis, C. I. (1918b). *A Survey of Symbolic Logic* (1st ed.). Berkeley: University of California Press.

Łukasiewicz, J. (1967a). On determinism (translation of o determiniźmie). In S. McCall (Ed.), *Polish Logic: 1920-1939*, pp. 19–39. Oxford.

Łukasiewicz, J. (1967b). Philosophical remarks on many-valued systems of propositional logic (translation of 'philosophische bemerkungen zu mehrwertigen systemen des ausagenkalküls'). In S. McCall (Ed.), *Polish Logic: 1920-1939*, pp. 40-65. Oxford.

MacColl, H. (1903). Symbolic reasoning v. *Mind (N.S.) 12*, 355-364.

MacColl, H. (1906). Symbolic reasoning vii. *Mind (N.S.) 15*, 504-518.

Mill, J. S. (1865). *Examination of Sir William Hamilton's Philosophy*. London.

Quine, W. V. O. (1953). Three grades of modal involvement. In *Actes du XI Congrès International de Philosophie, Bruxelles*, Volume 14, Amsterdam, pp. 65-81.

Rosser, J. B. and A. R. Turquette (1952). *Many-valued Logics*. Amsterdam: North Holland Publishing Co.

Russell, B. (1912). *The problems of philosophy* (Galaxy edition (1959) ed.). Oxford.

Schotch, P., B. Brown, and R. Jennings (Eds.) (2009). *On Preserving*. Toronto: University of Toronto Press.

Schotch, P. K. (2000). Skepticism and epistemic logic. *Studia Logica 65*, 187-198.

Schotch, P. K. and G. Payette (2011). Worlds and times. *Synthese*, 295-315.

Scott, D. (1973). Background to formalization. In H. Leblanc (Ed.), *Truth, Syntax and Modality*, pp. 244-273. Amsterdam: North Holland Publishing Company.

Scott, D. (1974). Completeness and axiomatization in many-valued logics. In *Proceedings of the Tarski Symposium*, pp. 411-435. AMS.

Segerberg, K. (1971). *An Essay in Classical Modal Logic*, Volume I. Uppsala: Uppsala University Press.

Smith, H. B. (1934). Abstract logic or the science of modality. *Philosophy of Science 1*.

Tarski, A. and B. Jónsson (1951). Boolean algebra with operators
    i. *American Journal of Mathematics 73*, 891–939.

Thijsse, E. (1992). *Partial Logic and Knowledge Representation.*
    Delft: Eburon Publishers.

Thomason, S. K. (1977). Possible worlds and many truth values.
    Studia Logica XXXVII(2), 195–204.

www.ingramcontent.com/pod-product-compliance
Lightning Source LLC
Chambersburg PA
CBHW020857090426
42736CB00008B/409